ALSO BY PATRICIA KELLEY

Final Gifts: Understanding the Special Awareness,
Needs, and Communications of the Dying
(with Maggie Callanan)

COMPANION
TO GRIEF

Finding Consolation When
Someone You Love Has Died

Patricia Kelley

Simon & Schuster

SIMON & SCHUSTER
Rockefeller Center
1230 Avenue of the Americas
New York, NY 10020

Designed by Diane E. Dougal

Manufactured in the United States of America

1 3 5 7 9 10 8 6 4 2

Library of Congress Cataloging-in-Publication Data
Kelley, Patricia, date.
Companion to grief : finding consolation when
someone you love has died / Patricia Kelley.
p. cm.
Includes bibliographical references and index.
1. Grief. 2. Consolation. I. Title.
BF575.G7K45 1997
155.9'37—dc20   96-35159
CIP

ISBN 0-684-81432-3

The real names of members of Elizabeth Hafner's family are used throughout
this book. To protect the privacy of others who are mentioned, names and
identifying details have been changed.

The publisher gratefully acknowledges permission to reprint "When We
Remember Them," by Sylvan Kamens and Jack Riemer, from the *The New
Mahzor Hadash for the High Holy Days*, edited by Sidney Greenberg and
Jonathan D. Levine, ©1995 & 1978 by the Prayer Book Press of Media
Judaica, Bridgeport, CT.

Acknowledgments

I am very grateful to Lynn Blough, Bron Hafner, and Karen Dasker for allowing me to use Elizabeth's death and our grief to set the scene for this book. Their stories, and those of the many other people mentioned, help us relate facts and theories about grief to real-life experiences. Theories are road maps to help us understand with our minds. Stories offer glimpses of the feelings and reactions of people who grieve, to help us also understand with our hearts.

While writing this book, and throughout my life, I have had many companions in grief. Some have been company and support when I have been grieving. Others have been guides or fellow travelers on my journey of exploring ways to bring comfort and consolation to those who grieve. And some have filled both roles. Thank you to Elaine Tiller, who first involved me in bereavement training, to Linda Anderson, Catherine Bates, Mary Boyken, Ira Byock, Lynn Hainge, Peter Hays, James Lwanga, Lin Noyes, Mike Rock, Mike Sutton, and Judy Tatelbaum, who are just a few of these companions; there are hundreds more.

Special thanks to my terrific agent, Gail Ross. She, her assis-

Acknowledgments

tant, Howard Yoon, my editor, Bob Bender, and his assistant, Johanna Li, are consistently supportive, affirming, and just great!

Last, but never least, my thanks and love to David and Sara, my children and sources of joy and pride; to Wendell, my step-daughter and dear friend; and to Craig, my husband and companion in love and life.

IN LOVING MEMORY OF ELIZABETH JOAN HAFNER

Contents

Chapter 1

Elizabeth

THE calls began to come more frequently. They had been each weekend, then two or three times a week, and sometimes now there were several a day.

When Elizabeth went home from what would be her final hospital stay, her voice, which had always been soft, was very weak and somewhat hoarse. But even over the phone we could hear her pleasure and relief to be home again. Talking on the phone used much of her limited energy, so we spoke mainly with Bron, her husband. At first he too had sounded relieved and pleased, but gradually—in his increasingly frequent calls—we heard more anxiety and more questions.

"Some days she seems better, some days she's much worse. What do you think will happen?"

"What can we do to get her to eat more?"

"She's never wanted to talk about not getting better. Do you think we should try to make her face that possibility?"

"She's recovered before when no one expected her to. Could she do it again?"

"Is it too hard on the three boys to see her like this? Should we let them visit? What should we tell them?"

"Her friend called from Arizona to ask if this was a good time to come to see her; I didn't know what to say. What do you think?"

To me, these questions sounded very familiar. In more than sixteen years as a nurse and educator in hospice care, I had heard similar questions many times. But this time was different. This time the person asking the questions was my husband's brother, Bron, and the person who was so ill was Bron's wife, Elizabeth. In addition to our connection through our husbands, Elizabeth and I were friends, and we loved one another.

Elizabeth had had surgery for breast cancer eleven years earlier. Her regular checkups after the operation showed no signs of the cancer reappearing. It seemed that the cancer had been removed before it had had a chance to spread.

About three years ago she developed pain in her right shoulder. At first she attributed this to having taken a heavy carry-on bag on a recent trip. But the pain didn't go away. She then developed nausea and stomach pains, which were thought to be side effects of the pain relievers she had been prescribed. By Thanksgiving she was feeling really ill. The following week she went into the hospital for tests and there it was found that the breast cancer had returned in her liver and bones.

The picture looked grim, but Elizabeth was a fighter. She used a combination of chemotherapy, radiation, meditation, relaxation, prayer, and stubborn determination to buy three more years. During that time she didn't just survive: she lived and enjoyed her life. There were some special times—a trip to Hawaii with her husband, and a trip to Catalina with her daughter—but mainly she chose to just live her life as usual. She continued going to work; spending time with her husband, mother, and daughter; playing computer games with her grandsons or taking them out for pizza; and celebrating family occasions.

One way Elizabeth chose to cope during this time was by not letting the cancer become the focus of her interactions with other people. Sometimes, most often with her husband or with me, she spoke of her illness, but usually she chose not to. She didn't like to be asked about her health, saying that she didn't want others to think of her as a person who was ill. At times, this made it hard for others to know how she was doing or what they might say to her, but she needed to maintain her privacy and reserve.

A little less than a year before her death, she and I spent a long day together, talking, shopping, and having lunch. The only outward sign of her illness was a need to climb stairs slowly, one by one. We followed our day with a long evening of more talking, and among other topics, we talked about death. We discussed the near-death experience each of us had had, and shared our thoughts about what happens at the time of death and our beliefs about life after death. Elizabeth talked realistically about knowing that the cancer would eventually cause her death, but said she planned to be around to see the boys finish school. The boys—her three grandsons—were then two, six, and eight years old, and when Elizabeth said "finish school," she meant college!

Our conversation that evening was illustrative of Elizabeth's attitude: quite clear about the reality of her illness and prognosis, confident and serene in her beliefs about death and afterward, and determined not to let her illness and impending death interfere with getting on with her life.

Last December she became very ill and again was admitted to the hospital. It seemed unlikely that she would survive long, but maybe not surprisingly, she improved. Her condition—although still serious—became stable, and she wanted to go home.

And she did . . .

I had suggested a referral to a hospice program for assistance and support at home, but Elizabeth wasn't interested, saying it was "too soon for hospice." A visiting nurse she liked and respected came every week to monitor her condition and advise her husband and mother on how to take care of her.

My husband and I were planning to visit two weeks later, but when the phone calls became more frequent, we went right away. Craig would be a support to his brother, and my role, I thought, would be to facilitate the discussions about hospice care. Instead, I canceled my other plans and stayed.

Elizabeth died a week later.

In many ways it was a very good week and in other ways it was very difficult. Elizabeth deteriorated rapidly, becoming weaker and weaker every day. She had little if any physical pain because of her physician's wise use of narcotics, given regularly and in appropriate amounts. She had some times of anxiety— usually related to her growing realization that she was becoming weaker. Swelling of her feet, legs, and abdomen made it difficult for her to move. We had to lift her gently out of bed to a chair, and even with help she could only shuffle a few steps. She had little appetite, which was not surprising. Usually, as a person gets closer to death the body's desire and need for food diminishes as part of a general slowing-down process. Elizabeth had very little energy, gradually becoming less interested in people or conversation, but seemed content with the presence of the people she loved most: her husband, Bron; her mother, Lynn; and her daughter, Karen.

The nights were the worst times. People who are dying often become restless or anxious at night, and Elizabeth's anxiety, although minimal, was more evident at night and was compounded by the physical effect of the feedings that were dripped through her veins during the night. Her diseased liver and weakened kidneys were not able to cope well with the fluid, and her body was swollen up to the level of her breasts. The extra fluid distending her abdomen and putting pressure against her diaphragm made it harder for her lungs to expand, so her breathing was labored, in spite of oxygen, and she was unable to lie down.

During her last night we stopped the feeding, and for the rest of that night and all through the following day she was very quiet, restful, and apparently at peace. She managed a few smiles, but no words, and by early afternoon she was not responding. Lynn, Bron, and I took turns cleansing her mouth gently with soft sponges, putting vitamin E oil on her lips, and changing the tapes so Elizabeth's favorite music continued to play softly. In between, Lynn kept busy—making a few phone calls, doing a little laundry, and folding nightgowns—while Bron spent most of the afternoon lying on the bed beside Elizabeth, holding her hand and talking to her about their lives together.

At about seven o'clock Lynn came into the bedroom to encourage Bron and me to go have something to eat. But as we left the room she called us back, because she thought Elizabeth was changing. She was right. Elizabeth's breathing pattern was changing, becoming deeper, slower, and more irregular. In a few more minutes, her breathing became very quiet, barely perceptible, then slowed even further and stopped. The three of us were with Elizabeth as she died.

•

In the days following her death, in between making arrangements, planning a memorial service, and doing all the other things that had to be done, my brother-in-law asked about grief. We had several discussions about grieving and mourning and what it might be like for him.

He asked me to recommend a book, and I gave him two or three that I thought would be helpful. But like most of us when we are grieving, he didn't have the energy or concentration to read much, and he couldn't find everything he needed in one book. So during the months which followed, I wrote him a series of letters about grief. These letters were his companion in his grief and form the basis of this book.

Like my brother-in-law, most people don't have much knowledge of the process of grieving. Some have misconceptions of what to expect, and many do not know how to find comfort and healing for their sadness. People have similar experiences when they grieve, but each person grieves differently, and many grieve alone.

When someone we love dies, any conversations about the death and our grief are often brief and uncomfortable, if they happen at all. We receive and respond to messages from ourselves and from others to be strong, to get over it quickly, and to avoid making others uncomfortable with our grief.

Most of us do not get over our grief quickly. Many people do not understand why—no matter how distressed they were at the time of the death—they feel worse a month or two later. Some feel guilty because they're angry at the one who died, some are embarrassed by sudden tears that come months, or even years, later, and some are exhausted by the abrupt and unpredictable changes in their moods and reactions.

Some people wonder if their grieving is abnormal. Are they taking too long? Should they be over it by now? Are they crying too much or too little? Would others be shocked because they feel greatly relieved that the person died? Do others notice that they can't concentrate? What would people think if they knew she sleeps cuddling her dead husband's sweater? What would they think if they knew he talks aloud to his dead wife while standing in the clothes closet, breathing in the lingering scent of her perfume?

Many people who are grieving feel very alone, even abandoned. They miss the person who died and often feel less connected to others in their lives. No others, no matter how close and no matter how similar their experiences, can understand how they feel. No one will go though grief in the same way.

For some, the intensity of their sadness, anger, or isolation, may be unexpected and overwhelming. For many, the inability to concentrate or to make decisions may be disconcerting and add to their distress. Most will feel uncertain about what is happening to them and how they can handle it.

•

This book will help you understand what is happening to you when you grieve. It gives you information in small amounts and in nonclinical language, and is designed to help anyone who is grieving the death of a spouse, another family member, or a friend or colleague. The letters I wrote to Bron have been shortened for the book, and each serves as an introduction to the specific aspect of grief addressed in the chapter it precedes. The material I omitted from the letters was focused on Bron and Elizabeth's particular circumstances. That material is incorporated into the chapters, along with additional information addressing issues that were not relevant to Bron but will be to many others.

All of us, when we grieve, need to know what is happening and what might help us. This is true for people who grieve within a loving family and for those whose family members are absent, estranged, or struggling in ways that add to their grief. We may need support when the person who died had a good life and a good death; we may need support when the life and death were miserable and full of suffering or full of inflicting pain on others. We may need support when our sadness at the death is mitigated by memories of a warm and loving relationship; we may need support when the relief we feel because of the death is accompanied by guilt, anger, or the memories of a difficult or abusive relationship.

•

Elizabeth's family, especially her husband, Bron; her mother, Lynn; her daughter, Karen; and I, hope you find this book helpful. In memory of Elizabeth we offer it to those who are grieving.

Chapter 2

Remembering

Dear Bron,

We reached home safely last night, and by the time this letter reaches you, no doubt Craig will have called you. We were both extremely tired, probably from all the emotions as well as the physical activity. I think you are probably much more tired than we are, or maybe you haven't noticed yet.

It's hard to believe that just two weeks ago we were arriving there to spend a weekend with you and Elizabeth. It seems so long ago, and so much has happened since then.

It's difficult to believe how weak she became so quickly, and it's painful to remember how hard she struggled. Even though she lived longer than anyone expected, we know she wanted longer.

I have some wonderful memories which I'm sure will always stay with me. I can still see Lynn cutting up oranges, which were about all Elizabeth wanted to eat or drink, and finding the right scrunchy to hold Elizabeth's hair—of course it had to match whichever nightdress we had helped her put on! And I was so touched by Karen and her love and gentleness as she cuddled in the bed, reading softly to her mother.

Then there was that morning a few days before Elizabeth died. She was really struggling that day, and at one point I said to her, "This seems like such hard work for you. We want to do whatever you want, so we're trying to support you in fighting this. But if you get too tired and want to stop fighting, please tell us. We'll understand."

"I'm ready now," she said.

"Ready for what?" I asked—rather stupidly, right?

"Ready to stop fighting this."

We hugged each other tearfully for a while and then I asked if she would like anything.

"Like what . . . ?" she asked.

"Well, maybe to see a priest . . . ?" I suggested. No, she and God didn't need any go-between. I asked if she wanted to talk to you . . . .

"About what?" she said.

"About not fighting this anymore."

"Oh, I'm going to keep fighting," she said with a grin, and even though we still had tears on our cheeks, we both laughed. Each time I think of her saying that, I find myself smiling and crying again. It was so typical of Elizabeth!

Over and over again, I hear you telling me about one of the special moments you had. I know you won't ever forget this, but I have to write it down to honor her memory. Was it two days before she died? You were holding Elizabeth in your arms as she sat on the side of the bed. She opened her eyes and saw that your eyes were full of tears.

"Don't do that," she said.

"What should I do?" you asked.

"Just stay by my side and love me."

I know that there have been very painful times for you throughout Elizabeth's illness, and that there will be many more as you start to work through the grief of living without her now. But I hope that you can find comfort in knowing that you did everything you could to help her, to keep her comfortable, to let her control as much as she could as long as she could, and to let her know how much you loved her. In the best possible way, even though it was difficult and painful, you did stay by her side and love her, and surely her dying was made easier for her by that.

You have tried to thank me for my help, and I appreciate your thanks, although I neither need nor expect them. But I also thank you and thank Elizabeth that I was able to be there during this time. It was a privilege to be with Elizabeth—during the difficult times, during the times of peace and comfort, and especially when she died so quietly and easily. I will never forget what a strong, loving, wonderful woman she was and is.

Craig and I talk about you often with love and concern. We'll be calling and writing to you, of course, but we hope that you will call us whenever you feel sad or lonely or whatever. Don't worry about the time, just call whenever you wish—day or night, east coast time or west coast time—one of us will surely be awake!

Lots of love,

IMMEDIATELY after someone you love dies, you may have a sense of everything seeming unreal. You may feel that time is somehow distorted: recent incidents seem distant, and events from long ago feel fresh and vivid.

Many people find themselves reliving incidents and moments

they shared with the one who died. You may find yourself going over and over the same incident in your mind, or aloud. Reliving, reviewing, and remembering these incidents and moments, however difficult and painful, can help you through your grief.

You may want to talk with others about these memories, or you may not. Some people are very uncomfortable talking about how they feel about the death and their grief. You may fear that you might cry, or feel that you don't want to bother others, or that there is something so very intimate about your grief that you need to keep it private.

You may find that you are particularly preoccupied with difficult memories. Perhaps you had an argument one morning and he had a heart attack later that day. Maybe you knew the car brakes needed attention but had forgotten to tell her, so you blame yourself for her death in a multiple-car pileup on a busy highway.

You may find yourself going over the details of what you know or imagine it was like for the person who died. This can be awful if the death was violent, such as a murder or a suicide, or if a death from natural causes was accompanied by massive bleeding or severe pain.

You may find that people don't want you to talk about the details of the death, especially any guilt or sense of responsibility you may feel about it, or any horror you may feel about how it happened. Sometimes people try to reassure you or distract you, thinking they're sparing you further pain.

Any and all of these reactions are common and can be expected. They might even be called normal, although often *nothing* about how you feel when you grieve feels normal. But there certainly isn't *one* way you should feel, should react, or should behave.

When you are distressed, other people sometimes think they should persuade or cajole you into behaving in a way they believe will help you but that you feel goes against all your instincts and wishes. Try to figure out what you want rather than what others want for you.

Be easy on yourself. This is a difficult time.

Points to Remember

- Expect to feel tired, even exhausted.
- Many things may seem unreal.
- Time may seem to be altered, and you may wonder if something happened yesterday, last week, or ages ago.
- You may find yourself constantly reliving moments and incidents you shared with the person who died.
- You may find it helpful to talk with others and reminisce about the person who died.
- You may feel reluctant to talk with anyone about the person who died.
- Be gentle with yourself.

from grief means forgetting someone they love. Everyone grieves somewhat differently, but most of us feel and react to loss in similar ways.

Common Reactions and Feelings

You will probably find that grief brings many different emotions. You may feel sad, guilty, angry, lonely, abandoned, isolated, numb, bewildered, relieved. Some people find it difficult to identify or understand their reactions, especially if they're feeling numb. Someone I know said he felt so cold and numb that it was as though he had died as well.

You may feel two or more emotions at the same time. If you have ever waited and waited for someone who is very late, you know how your concern or irritation can escalate into anxiety and fear that something dreadful has happened. When that person arrives you're relieved and thankful, *and* at the same time you're resentful and angry, especially if they could have let you know they'd be late.

Similarly, when you are grieving you may find yourself feeling two seemingly incompatible emotions simultaneously. Maybe you feel glad the person is no longer in pain—and angry that she left you. You may feel grateful for the assistance of your family—and at the same time irritated by their presence.

You may find your moods shift frequently and abruptly. Perhaps you're calmly planning a service and suddenly feel overcome with sadness and tears. You may be feeling extremely depressed and then find yourself laughing at something funny. This emotional roller coaster seems to drain your energy.

You may feel relief that the person has died, that he is no longer suffering, and that any fears about what awful things *might* happen weren't realized. You also may find yourself furious with someone who suggests that you might be feeling relieved! You're glad he's not suffering, but why couldn't the end of his suffering have been a cure and return to health rather than death? You may feel angry, perhaps at yourself, at friends who kept their distance, at people who tell you how to feel and what to do, at those who helped you, even at the one who died for dying and leaving you.

You may have times when you are overcome by sadness and can't stop crying.

Liz said: "All that first day, and for hours every day in the weeks that followed, I cried and sobbed. I even screamed and screamed at God that he couldn't let this happen, that I couldn't stand it, that there was no way I could survive."

There may also be times when you seem quite detached from the pain and are able to function apparently as usual. Sometimes you may forget or not believe that the person died.

Sonia said: "I've known for months she was dying. Every day during these last few weeks I've seen her get closer and closer to death. But now that she's dead, I don't believe it. Even when I say 'She's dead,' those words make no sense to me."

You may feel guilty. This is common whether or not there is any reason for guilt. You may wonder what you could have done differently: Could you have been gentler, more patient, or more understanding? Should you have changed your whole life for the last few years?

You may experience a change in your eating or sleeping habits. You may find yourself eating too much or too little or sleeping too much or too little. You may feel exhausted and yet have difficulty sleeping. You may wish everyone would go away and stop bothering you, or you may find yourself clinging to people and dreading being alone.

Some people find that grief causes physical pain—perhaps a headache, a backache, or a feeling of emptiness inside. The term "brokenhearted" may suddenly seem very real to you, because your heart feels broken, hurt, and aching.

Darrell said: "Her death feels like there's a sword being driven through my belly—it hurts so much and it's tearing me apart. And when I think I can't stand the pain anymore, the sword twists and hurts even more."

You may feel physically ill. You may catch every virus that's going around, or, if you have a chronic illness, it may be exacerbated by your grief.

You may find yourself going over and over in your mind what happened, perhaps hoping that you can find a better ending. You may see or hear the person who died; some people say they are afraid that this means they must be "going crazy." In fact, this is a fairly common occurrence for grieving people— over half of grieving spouses say it has happened to them.

Most of us have some difficulty concentrating or remembering when we are grieving. Perhaps you will have bursts of energy and start a project, either at home or at work, and then find that the energy is short-lived and that you cannot concentrate on the project or cannot even remember what it is you're supposed to be doing. For many of us, making decisions becomes difficult or even impossible. This doesn't just apply to big decisions—I think most of us can understand why conventional wisdom advises those who are grieving not to make major decisions at first. But even little, everyday decisions— what to wear, what to eat, the process of getting up and going to work—can be difficult too.

I sometimes think of our emotions when we grieve as being like a kaleidoscope—where many little pieces of shapes and colors form patterns that change with any movement. The various emotions may come separately in rapid succession or several may come at the same time, and when something changes, they all shift. Because each shift may cause more pain, it is no wonder that grief may be overwhelming.

Grief Is Both Familiar and Strange

Grief is a natural reaction to loss, and loss is a part of everyone's life. We all experience the loss of relationships, opportunities, or material possessions. As children we may lose a favorite toy, a pet, or a special teacher. Later we may lose a job, or a home, or a spouse through divorce. Our children grow up and move away; we lose our youth, perhaps our looks, and sometimes our dreams. These losses are part of life and we learn to adjust.

But when someone you love dies, either suddenly in an accident or after a long, difficult struggle with illness, there are many losses to cope with—and all at the same time. When you lose a parent, spouse, child, sibling, or friend, in addition to the individual you lose the roles that person played in your life, and, most important, you lose the relationship you had with one another. You lose the activities you shared in the past and the plans you made together for the future. No wonder the grief can seem so hard.

Because grief is part of life, it may seem familiar and at the same time very strange. Many people find talking about grief or death to be awkward and less than satisfying, if they talk about it at all. Many people have few, if any, role models from whom they can learn helpful ways to grieve. Many have little information about the process of grieving and how to get through it. Having an understanding of what happens to us as we grieve does not take away the pain, but it can help make the process somewhat easier.

Some people find it helpful to compare grief to being on a journey and suddenly losing the map. Where am I? Where am I going? How do I get there? Where have I been? It can feel like being lost. We keep asking the questions to which there are no answers, but we ask them again anyway.

Grieving is in fact a journey—a journey toward healing the pain caused by our loss. To reach the point where we feel whole again we cannot go around our grief, we cannot avoid it, we cannot ignore it. To find healing for our pain we must make our way *through* our grief. Being clear about this destination can help you plan your journey and adjust to setbacks and difficulties you will encounter and overcome.

Because everyone grieves differently, there are no exact directions for this journey, but there is a great deal of useful information available. We know what factors may affect the way we grieve, how long healing might take, what work we need to do along the way, how other people may help or hinder our progress, and what has helped others.

Points to Remember

- Grief is a natural response to loss.
- Grief is a painful process—try to be patient with yourself and with the process.
- When the sadness seems overwhelming, remind yourself that you will journey through it.
- Your destination is to feel whole again.
- Take good care of yourself.

Chapter 4

How Long Will This Go On?

Dear Bron,

It's one month today since Elizabeth died. To me it sometimes seems like yesterday, sometimes feels like ages ago, and sometimes feels as if it didn't really happen. How about you?

You asked how long your grief will last. I'm afraid I'm going to give you my usual answer—as with many other questions about grieving, there is no single answer. The length of time varies from one person to another, and from one loss to another. However, I can give you some general idea of how long it takes most people.

It will probably take you about a year or two to complete most of your grieving. That doesn't mean you'll have a whole year or two years of feeling the way you do now. Nor does it mean that you'll be completely over your grief after a year or two. Sometimes it may seem as though you're moving along well, and at other times you may feel you're not making any progress at all, or even that you're going backward.

It may be helpful to think of grieving as a three-part

process. Throughout the time you're grieving, you'll experience similar reactions and feelings, but in each of the three parts some of these reactions will be stronger and more frequent.

The most common reactions in the first month or two after a death have to do with disbelief: we react with shock and denial. During the month since Elizabeth died, have there been times when you haven't believed it really happened? I certainly have had moments of not quite believing it.

You'll probably find that the reality of her death will really sink in during the next few months. As the shock and disbelief begin to wear off you may find other feelings, such as sadness, anger, loneliness, depression, and emptiness, are more intense and more prolonged. They may even seem to completely consume you.

After another few months you'll still have some feelings of disbelief and also periods of sadness, but they will gradually start to diminish. You may feel them less frequently or less intensely. You'll probably find you have more energy and enthusiasm and are able to concentrate and plan ahead, and you'll gradually notice that you're feeling better.

So your grief may last a year or two, or maybe longer, although for various reasons I think it may be shorter.

You'll probably find the next few months the hardest. If you start to feel worse, try to remind yourself that this is another step in the journey of grieving, and that going through it will help you reach healing. Please lean on those of us who love you, and please take good care of yourself.

Lots of love,

GRIEVING the death of someone you love typically takes longer than you might expect. Most people don't think their grieving will last as long as a year. It may take you a year or two or even longer to feel that your grieving is over. It's important to remember that if you grieve for a long time, it doesn't mean there's something wrong with you. It means you need more time to grieve fully so that you can heal fully. Try to be patient with yourself.

And in some ways your grief may never be finished, just changed. You won't forget the person who died and the relationship you shared, but you'll come to a grudging acceptance of the death and your loss and a realization that you have to go on. As you adjust and the grief changes, it becomes a part of you and a part of your life.

Stages of Grief

Many people have heard about stages of dying and/or stages of grieving. Friends and family members may even ask you which one you're in. This can be confusing, since there are several lists that include anywhere from five to nine separate stages. You may also find it misleading, because the word "stages" may suggest that you'll make a neat, orderly progression from one phase to another. The stages describe our reactions to the death of someone we love, and usually those reactions are not neat and orderly.

Through extensive reading and practical experience over the years, I've pared these lists to just three stages: *disbelief, pain,* and *healing.*

Though these three stages share some of the same emotions—sadness, anger, depression, loneliness, shock, emptiness, relief, fear for the future, etc.—each one is named for the feeling that dominates in frequency and intensity.

Disbelief: During the first month or so your strongest reactions will probably be related to shock and disbelief. You may find yourself thinking or saying, "This can't be true." You may wake up in the morning forgetting that the whole thing happened. You may pick up the phone to call her, or set his place at the table for dinner. And each time you "forget" that the person you loved died, there will be fresh pain as you remember.

Disbelief is a common response in all of us to any bad news—we don't *want* to believe it. This stage of shock allows the truth to sink in more slowly, in small doses, and helps us adjust gradually to the full impact of the pain. This disbelief may last the first three to seven weeks.

Pain: The second stage is when the disbelief and shock are wearing off, when your reactions relate mainly to the painful realization that she or he has indeed died. In the first stage, you experienced some feelings of sadness, depression, anger, and loneliness. But now, without the protection of numbness or shock, these feelings will be more intense, more prolonged, and can seem overwhelming; you may feel like everything is falling apart. This stage may last about four months.

Healing: During this third stage, you'll still have some moments of disbelief and feelings of sadness, but you'll find that feelings associated with healing from grief become stronger and occur more often. You'll have more interest in what is going on around you—in work, at home, with your family—and you'll feel more energetic and enthusiastic. You'll be able to concentrate for longer periods of time and even be able to plan ahead.

For most people, there is no specific point at which they can say, "Now I'm recovered." Rather, there is a gradual recognition of these signs of healing, and a realization of a readiness again to become fully involved in living. This stage of reorganization also may last about four months.

Recognizing these three parts can help you understand your varying emotions, but don't expect to finish stage one and move to stage two, finish stage two and move to stage three.

The stage only indicates which emotion is strongest at that time; we still feel many other emotions during each stage. Most of us go back and forth and in and out of these stages, experiencing many reactions and emotions in the process. Often it's only when we look back that we see some indication of when the changes happened, when we were feeling *mostly* disbelief, *mostly* pain, or *mostly* healing.

Progress through this three-part process is usually very gradual and sometimes barely perceptible. It's also very individual; no two people will progress in the same way at the same pace. You'll probably find your reactions and emotions shift frequently throughout your grieving. Don't expect your grief to follow a schedule, and don't worry about what stage you are in.

Especially Difficult Times

Although everyone grieves differently, it will help you to be aware of some commonly difficult times, so you can be prepared.

1. *About one month* after the death, many people become quite concerned because they don't seem to be feeling any better. This is because the shock which numbed their pain has begun to wear off, so they do in fact feel worse. At about the same time they may notice that they seem to be receiving less support from others, who think that by now they are "over the worst of it."

Susan's father died at eighty-three, peacefully and quietly after a long illness. Susan, her mother, and her sisters had expected his death and had followed his wishes for the services.

Susan had wept quietly after her father's death and at the funeral, but mainly she felt relieved that his long, debilitating illness was over.

"About five weeks after he died, I was driving home from work, and I heard on the radio a piece of music which he loved. I started to cry, and soon I was crying so hard that I couldn't see properly so I pulled off the road. It was about fifteen minutes before I could get myself together and drive the rest of the way home. That was two weeks ago, and I've been crying on and off ever since. I feel so sad and I miss him so much. I really didn't expect this."

Like Susan, you may feel relief when someone dies, especially if it's an elderly person dying peacefully after a long illness. Also, like Susan, you may not realize that you have other feelings as well as relief, and sometimes it takes a while to recognize the sadness. It often comes as a surprise that grief becomes worse, not better. But this is understandable: as the shock and disbelief wear off, you'll feel more of the pain and sadness.

2. *About four to six months* after the death, many people feel very depressed, and may wonder if they will ever be better.

Sam was forty-one when his wife died, leaving him and two children under ten. During Janet's illness, Sam had utilized all the support he could find: he had arranged for her to be driven to radiation treatments by volunteers from the American Cancer Society. In addition, ACS gave him a hospital bed. The local hospice helped Sam and Janet plan and manage her care, and provided counseling for the children, both before and after her death; and their church helped with prayers, companionship, and casseroles. Throughout Janet's illness, Sam had refused offers of support for himself and seemed to be very self-sufficient.

He was contacted by the hospice bereavement counselor two weeks after Janet's death and again after three months. On each of these occasions, he thanked the person for calling and declined any offers of support, or opportunities to join a grief group. He said he was doing fine.

Six months after her death Sam was contacted again. He talked with the counselor for an hour and a half on the phone, met with her for an individual counseling session a few days later, and then attended a six-week grief group. Much later he spoke about how the bereavement team seemed to be able to read his mind:

"How did they know when I needed help? I'd been doing so well, I thought I was all over Janet's death. Then I just lost it— I couldn't eat, or sleep, or work, or pay attention to the kids, and that was the week they called me.

"How did they know to keep offering support even when I had told them so many times that I was fine? I was feeling so low at that point, I couldn't have picked up the phone to ask them or anyone else to help me.

"How did they know that what I needed was to talk to someone who could understand what was going on without telling me to snap out of it or to be strong?

"How did they know that when the group ended after six weeks I would realize that my reactions were normal, that I would recover, and that I had met three people in my group whom I could call on—and I did—at times when I felt bad?"

3. *Any day of special meaning* to you and the one who died will also stir up memories, which may increase your sadness. These days might be the person's birthday, your birthday, wedding anniversaries, national and religious holidays, and the anniversary of the day of death.

Marian was twenty-seven when her husband was killed in a traffic accident. She had good support from her family and friends, and felt she was getting through her grief as well as possible.

"The morning after the first anniversary of his death I woke up feeling terrible, and lay in bed trying to figure out why I felt so bad. I realized that in some way I had thought I'd be grieving for a year and then I'd be better. The first year was over, but I wasn't better. In fact, I felt worse."

When asked what she had done on the anniversary of his death, she replied, "I tried to keep busy so I wouldn't dwell on it. Several people told me later they'd been thinking of me but hadn't called or said anything because they didn't want to remind me—as if I could forget!"

Following a few sessions with a grief counselor, she planned how she would cope with her wedding anniversary. "I'm not going to pretend that it's just another day. It isn't. I'm going to church with his mother in the morning, and we'll take flowers to his grave and have lunch together. Then I'm going to have a quiet dinner with the couple who were our best friends. It'll be hard, and I'm sure I'll cry and be sad. But I'll also laugh and remember some of the good times. And I'll be with people who love him like I do."

At times like these when your grieving seems particularly difficult to endure, you may find it helpful to seek out more support, perhaps a grief group. In a later chapter we'll focus on when and how to find support, including grief groups and counseling.

Making Progress

Grieving is a gradual process, with sometimes barely perceptible changes. It often helps to remember this and to find ways to appreciate the progress you make, no matter how small or slow it seems. Some people keep a journal and find the little day-by-day changes are more noticeable when they reread several weeks' worth of entries. Some people join a grief group, which can help in many ways, including allowing them to discuss their progress during the six to eight weeks that most grief groups last. Others find they benefit from regular weekly attendance at a support group for many months.

At times, maybe often, you'll wonder if you're going the wrong way on this journey. To extend the metaphor, you may be reminded of when you've been given directions to a place by someone who says, "You can't miss it." Many of us find that we can and do "miss it." Although explanations of the process of grieving do give us some comfort by enabling us to understand what is going on, those explanations may also seem like the directions that are supposed to be so simple that "we can't miss." In reality, we'll probably find it takes us a long time and several wrong turns as we stumble along this journey.

Time Alone Won't Heal

You may have met people who claim to be "all over it" after a matter of a few weeks or months, and you may have met people who seem to have made no progress in grieving even several years later. People may tell you that time heals—and sometimes it seems that way. Most of us can remember times when we felt so bad that we thought we'd never feel better, but eventually we did.

People often have different reactions to being told that time will heal their pain. Some want to hear it because they want to be convinced that they will feel better. Some may be angry, because even if it's true, it doesn't alleviate their misery at the moment. Others may find it impossible to believe they will ever feel better.

Time alone cannot heal your grief; there is also work to do. Completing the work, or tasks, of grieving leads to healing. Considering these tasks will help you understand your reactions to the death and better identify those things that will help you

recover from your grief. If you don't complete this grief work, the wounds may never heal, no matter how much time passes.
The next several chapters describe these tasks.

Points to Remember

- No one knows how long you will grieve.
- Grief takes time and work!
- There are three parts to grief: *disbelief, pain,* and *healing.*
- For many people, the worst grief comes four to six months after the death.
- Expect that special days and events may trigger emotional reactions and plan how you prefer to handle them.
- Time alone won't heal your grief.
- There is much to do and progress may be slow, but you can work through it.
- Seek help from friends, family, a grief counselor, and/or a support group.

Chapter 5

Grieving Is Hard Work

Dear Bron,

I'm glad to hear you're letting Mark take on extra responsibilities at work for a while. Maybe that'll take some pressure off you. You've sounded very tired on the phone the last few days, so this letter should be timely.

Many people who are grieving say they're always tired or don't seem to have any energy. In fact, grieving is hard work. You're working on several tasks that will take you through the process of grieving to reach healing. You're tired because these tasks require physical and emotional energy—like most work.

Much of what happened recently that has contributed to your fatigue will actually help you with these tasks. Obviously there's physical fatigue from taking care of Elizabeth, but there's emotional exhaustion also. And what has caused that exhaustion has already helped you complete some of your grief work.

You were with Elizabeth throughout her illness and almost every moment of that last week. In those last few days and nights, you saw her last few smiles, heard her last few words, and were with her when she took her last breaths. You sat with her after she died, called the funeral home, saw her body leave your home for the last time, planned the service. Much of what you did with and for Elizabeth was emotionally painful.

However, much of what you did was also grief work. You were working on the tasks that help you move through the grief to where you can find healing. I've attached some material about the tasks of grieving for you to read when you feel like it.

For now, try to remember that if you feel tired it shouldn't be surprising. Grieving can be as tiring as any other work. It's especially important to take good care of yourself now. Are you eating wisely and getting enough exercise and rest? I know you've been attending church more, and I hope that's bringing you some peace.

We'll talk to you soon.

Love,

MANY people who are grieving find they have no energy and always feel tired. Sometimes it feels as if you have labored all day, although you have accomplished very little. Grieving *is* hard work. In fact, counselors often refer to the grieving process as "grief work." They agree that it's helpful to consider just what is the work you're doing and how you are doing it.

The purpose of grieving is not to forget the person who died or to diminish the importance of your relationship. Rather, it is a process through which you will find healing of most of your emotional pain from your loss. This process requires you to complete a series of tasks.

Tasks of Grieving

Several well-respected psychologists have described the tasks of grieving. I have found the work of William Worden, who defined four tasks, particularly helpful. Erich Lindemann described three, and Parkes and Weiss also identified three. These researchers defined the work of grieving in essentially similar ways.

In my experience, the work of grieving can be considered as completing the following three tasks:

1. To believe the death really happened.
2. To experience the pain of the grief.
3. To learn to live without the person who died.

What does all this mean and how does it apply to what you go through when you grieve? Some might say that the first and third tasks are obvious—they know the death happened, and they are learning to live without the person who died. Most people would probably prefer to avoid the second task if they could.

To understand the work required to complete these tasks is to understand why grieving takes so much physical and emotional energy. You won't work on each task separately—many of your experiences will relate to two or more tasks. However, examining each task separately can help you understand your reactions and discover what might help you reach a place where you feel healed.

This chapter looks at the first task of grieving.

The First Task: To Believe the Death Really Happened

What does it mean to believe the death really happened, to accept the reality of the loss? It means you need to reach a point where you *know and believe* that the person you love is dead and will not return. Of course, you already know this, at least somewhat. But it often takes months to fully absorb and believe it. You may know it on an intellectual level at first and take longer to know it on an emotional level.

To complete this task, you need to gather evidence to overcome your instinctive and understandable wish not to believe that the person you love is dead. If you gathered at least some of the information before the death, you have already started on this task; if not, you need to do the necessary work now. How much you need to do can vary, depending upon many factors.

Sudden vs. Expected Deaths

If the death was expected—if you knew the person was very old or seriously ill—you may have considered the possibility that he or she might die and have begun working on this task before the death. If the death was sudden—perhaps the person had a heart attack without warning or was killed in a traffic accident—you begin this task only after the time of death. Naturally, it often takes longer to accept the reality of the death if it was unexpected.

Amy was in her early forties and was distraught when her mother was killed in a car accident.

"I can't deal with this, it can't be true, I didn't have any warning! I didn't get to say goodbye, and we had a fight last week when she told me I was bossy. Now we can't make up!"

Amy's grief seemed worse partly because she was comparing her reactions to her mother's death to her reactions after the death of her father several years before. He had died of cancer, and the whole family had helped care for him at home. They had taken the opportunities to tell their father how much they loved him and how much they'd miss him. Several times they had looked at old photos and reminisced about times when Amy and her three brothers were young. These conversations were sometimes tearful, sometimes hilarious, and always healing.

What Amy went through with her father is called *anticipatory grieving*. Anticipating the approaching death and how it will affect you allows you to begin your grieving before the person dies. By the time her father died, Amy had completed a great deal of the work of the first task. However, when her mother died suddenly, Amy had to begin *all* the work of that task.

Awareness of the Person's Illness

If you have prolonged contact with someone very ill, you watch that person become weaker and sicker. By observing this deterioration, you gradually absorb the reality of the serious illness and the possibility of death. In some cases, you may have known the person was ill but had been told it was a minor illness and not life-threatening. Or you may have been told nothing at all. No matter what the actual cause of death, your reactions will depend upon whether *you* see the death as sudden or expected.

Bill, twenty-six, liked to say that the slogan "Peace Corps: the toughest job you'll ever love" accurately described how he felt about his work as a Peace Corps volunteer in West Africa. Stationed in a small village twelve hours by bus from the nearest city, he worked in an agricultural program and often compared his experiences in the village with growing up in a small farming community in the American Midwest.

Bill was one of seven siblings in a family he described as "just great." He always enjoyed getting mail from home. About a year after he arrived in Africa, the letters from home suddenly stopped; and there were none for more than a month. He made his way into the city and phoned home to ask what was going on.

"They said everything was fine, but they hadn't written because everyone was so busy. I talked to everyone except Dad because he'd had a cold and a little bronchitis. Mom said he was better now, but still a little hoarse, so she didn't want him to get on the phone and talk too much."

About six weeks later, one of the Peace Corps staff traveled to Bill's village bringing a telegram from home. His father had died after being ill for two months with bronchitis and pneumonia, which had led to congestive heart failure. Bill seemed numb as the staff member helped him get his things together, took him into the city, and saw him onto the airplane that took him home.

When Bill returned to Africa after the funeral, he said, "I don't know which was worse: not knowing why they weren't writing to me, or having them tell me it wasn't serious. I know they meant well, they didn't want me to worry, but it was such a shock to find out that he'd been sick for several months. If I'd known, I would have written to him more, or called more. I might even have cut my time of service short and gone home early. I really don't know now what I'd have done, but I wish I could have had a choice."

Being Present at the Time of Death

Frequent contact with the dying person, family, friends, doctor, nurses, and others may help you absorb the implications of the changes which are happening as the person gets closer to death. If you are present at the time of death, it may help make death seem more real. If you spend some time sitting with the body afterward you'll notice some changes: the body becomes colder, and you may sense that the person is no longer in that body. These details can all help make death more real to you.

Rituals After Death

Were you present at the viewing, the funeral or service, the burial, or the cremation, or sprinkling of ashes? Did you attend a Mass of the Resurrection for a Catholic, sit shivah for a Jew, attend prayers on the thirtieth day for a Muslim, participate in a memorial service where people were invited to contribute a memory? These and other rituals that formally recognize and mourn the death reinforce its reality.

Other less formal rituals can also help. Phoning or visiting the home to offer condolences to the family may provide you a chance to hear more details. Evidence gathered by others can help you complete your picture of what happened.

Telling Your Story

Repeating the story of your loss is an important and very common need, and each story is as individual as the one who grieves. You and I may be grieving for the same person, but your story is different from mine because your relationship with the person was different from mine.

Your story may begin with a phone call telling you of a fatal accident, or with knowing he was ill but expecting him to recover, or with rushing to the hospital and spending hours or days praying desperately that she would survive.

You may tell the story aloud to friends or family, or silently in your mind to yourself, or to God in prayer. You may write the story, or parts of it, in letters to friends, or in a journal.

Some people feel uncomfortable with their need to tell the

story. You may worry that people have heard it a number of times and must be tired of it. If you feel the need to tell it again, consider finding a grief group or counselor.

Some people feel their grief is such an intimate experience that they can't share it with anyone else. Such individuals may choose to tell their story in a letter or journal, or talk it through in their minds or hearts. Some people find comfort in telling the story to the one who died—perhaps talking to a photograph or holding a special possession as they speak.

Telling the story of the death and your loss, in whatever way feels most comfortable for you, can be one of the most important ways to complete the tasks of grieving.

Mike was a young man whose friend Joe had just died. After a turbulent adolescence, Joe had decided to get his life in order. He had worked two jobs to support himself through the seven years it took him to finish college. Soon after completing his final exams, he fell asleep at the wheel of his old car, went off the road, and was killed.

As Mike was telling me what happened, he started to cry. He wept steadily for several minutes, and then said, "You know, every time I tell this story, I get a little bit farther before I start to cry."

This is not necessarily what happens literally, but it is an illustration of why we need to tell the story. Whenever we go over what happened, it becomes a little more real until we are able to believe the death did happen, and we progress a little farther in our journey through the pain and toward healing.

Understanding Your Experiences

You may wake up at night thinking you heard him call you, or you might glance up from the paper because you sensed she had come into the room. People sometimes find themselves approaching someone on the bus or subway, thinking for a moment it was the one who died, or they may pick up the phone, forgetting, as they dial the number of a now-disconnected telephone, that the person died.

Experiences such as these are part of grief. Each time you "forget" you will remember again, and each time you remember, you will feel the pain of your loss again. And each time you feel that pain, you will believe the reality a little more. Although this remembering helps you to work on the first and second tasks of grieving, it can be very distressing. "Forgetting" that someone you love dearly has died can be very upsetting, and seeing and hearing the person who died can feel very strange. You may start wondering if you're going crazy and need to talk with someone who can reassure you that these are common experiences.

Saying Goodbye

If you were not present before, after, or at the time of death, or if you were not at any of the services, you may find it helpful to find your own way to say goodbye. Perhaps you want to hold a religious service, or visit a place that was special to you both, or reread a book of poems he loved, or play her favorite piece of music. You might find it helpful to write a letter to the one who died, and either keep it or burn it in a ceremonial way.

Taking Care of Yourself

It is not uncommon for people who are grieving to neglect their own needs. Maybe you need to eat more wisely or get more rest or exercise. Perhaps you have a health problem that you have been neglecting because you were so concerned with the one who died. This is the time to do something for your physical health.

It is also important to consider your emotional and spiritual needs. In many societies it is common for groups of family members and friends to gather at the home of the person who died. We hope our presence shows respect for the one who died and concern for those who may be most affected by the death. At the same time, by sharing our grief, we often receive some emotional comfort. Maybe the pain of the loss of one person can be balanced a little by being with others who share our sadness. The hugs, tears, and reunions which are part of many funerals or memorial services show how we reach out for comfort from one another.

Many people who have a religious faith say they cannot imagine being able to cope with the death of someone they love without their faith. Religious rituals and traditions concerning death are usually focused on helping a dying person be prepared for death, and on handling of the body after death. Those same rituals can be very comforting to those who are grieving.

When a Muslim reads passages of the Koran to a dying person, he hopes that the word of God will be in the ears of the dying person. At the same time, the one who is reading may find comfort both from the words he reads and by performing this service.

Judaism may require specific ways of handling the body after death as a sign of respect for God and the one who died, but making sure the traditions are followed can bring comfort to the mourners.

Prayers and anointing with holy oils may be offered to help a Christian prepare for death and the next life. And participating in those prayers can bring comfort to the survivors.

For many people their religious faith offers important comfort for their grief, and the ministers of their faith, whether their ministry is formal or informal, are essential supports. Religions, and the traditions and people who represent them, offer spiritual comfort for many people—they help us find meaning at times when meaning may be hard to find.

But some people have no faith or interest in religion, and others feel estranged or excluded from traditional religion. The spiritual needs of those who are not interested in, or affiliated with, a specific religion are often ignored. People who have no religion do have spiritual needs related to finding meaning and comfort.

Those who find comfort in religion are sometimes inclined to offer their beliefs to others who do not share that faith. Although this is meant to offer comfort, it may cause more distress. Rather than telling a person what to believe, it is more helpful to assist that person to draw strength from his or her beliefs. Perhaps one of the most important questions we can ask someone who grieves is:

"Where do you find your spiritual strength, and how can you nurture this strength?"

Finding Help with This Task

Find someone you can talk to about your grief and sadness. This could be a member of your family, a friend, a grief counselor, or a pastoral counselor. It has to be someone who listens to you tell your story as often as you need to, helps you understand experiences that are a part of your grief, and is willing to keep you company. See the last chapter for ways to find support.

Points to Remember
_____

- Grief is hard work!
- Understanding the tasks of grieving can help you understand your reactions and your needs.
- The first task is to believe the death really happened.
- Many factors may affect how you work on and complete this first task.

Chapter 6

It Hurts

Dear Bron,

You seemed very sad when we talked last night. I agree with you—the pain of Elizabeth's death feels much worse now than when she died. As you said, now you really know that it happened and that hurts.

Although you knew Elizabeth was dying, there was probably some part of you that didn't quite believe it. As the shock and disbelief wear off now, her death will continue to feel more and more real to you and will cause you more pain. This is the hardest part of grieving.

Painful feelings are part of missing someone you love. If you could see that experiencing these feelings and reactions is one of your tasks of grieving, it might be easier to understand how your sadness, anger, and loneliness will help you get through your grief to find healing. However, although understanding what is happening can help on an intellectual level, it won't relieve your sadness.

I think you've already done some of the work of experiencing the pain of your loss. The pain at the time of Elizabeth's death, the emotions at the service and at the gathering we held in her honor afterward, the tears before and since her death, are all steps toward completing this task.

I understand what you said about well-meaning people who make you feel worse. Those who tell you not to keep dwelling on her death may seem to be ignoring your distress or suggesting that it's time you got over it. Those who say that Elizabeth wouldn't want you to be sad, that she'd want you to go on with your life, are probably trying to help. But you may feel they are judging you and even implying that you are somehow letting Elizabeth down.

It's often difficult to know how to respond to comments such as these. You might say simply, "Right now that doesn't help me, I'm too sad." You could even add, "I have to mourn for Elizabeth now so I can work through my grief." It is in fact easier to go on with life if we have worked through our grief.

When we're grieving, we all need people who let us know that they understand if we're sad, or if we don't feel like being sociable, or if we cry. I hope you continue to spend time with people who let you do this, and that you continue to talk with us.

When you are hurting so much, it may not be much comfort to know that it sounds to me as if you are making progress in working through your grief. Although it may feel awful, it is progress to move from disbelief to the pain of believing that Elizabeth died.

Love and peace,

———————————————

As we work to complete the first task of grieving—believing the death really happened—we're also working on the second task:

58

experiencing the pain of our grief. These two tasks are closely related. The more we accept the reality of the death, the more we experience the pain of our loss. The more we feel the pain, the more we believe he or she really did die. It may, and often does, take considerable time for us to absorb fully the reality and the finality of another's death. Maybe it would be too much to take all the pain at once, so we absorb a little at a time, and the enormity of our loss may not be felt for weeks or months.

Wanting to Avoid Pain

The sadness, depression, anger, loneliness, confusion, helplessness, guilt, and all the other emotions we may feel when someone we love dies can add up to a great deal of pain. Many of us would prefer not to feel this pain—instinctively and understandably we want to avoid anything in life that hurts us.

Trying to avoid those feelings doesn't seem to work. We may be able to delay facing them for a while, but eventually we will have to experience the pain of our grief. We cannot go around it or bypass it. There seems to be a certain portion of pain for every death. If we try to avoid that pain, it may resurface later in life—commonly when we're facing another loss. So when someone else whom we love dies, we may find our grief then is compounded by the earlier grief that we had tried to avoid.

When people take care of a dying family member, they often grieve in anticipation of that person's death. But sometimes they also begin the grief work for another person who died, sometimes even quite a long time ago. The second loss that triggers the grief may not be one that affects them directly.

Robert, the manager of a department in a large federal agency, made an appointment with a counselor in the Employee Assistance Program (EAP). He said he needed advice about an employee, Ben, whom he had supervised for several years. Ben had informed him that his cancer, which had been in remission, had now recurred and spread to several major organs in his body. The only available treatments were not expected to help, and he didn't know how much longer he would be able to work, or even be alive.

Robert told the EAP counselor he needed advice on how to help Ben and his coworkers and at the same time maintain productivity in his department. At first he focused on specific, concrete issues related to an employee with a serious illness, such as sick leave, how to provide reasonable accommodation, and when to suggest disability retirement. He and the counselor discussed these topics and various options, and then the counselor asked Robert how he was reacting to Ben's condition.

Robert frowned and looked at the counselor in silence for a few moments. Then he said. "This may seem strange, but when Ben told me about this I really didn't want to hear it. I tried to pay attention and be sympathetic, but I couldn't seem to concentrate on what he was saying—I wanted him to get out of my office."

Robert had been surprised by his reaction. Later he decided that in addition to feeling uncomfortable with the topic of serious illness, he was also anxiously wondering how he was going to manage without a key employee. But that afternoon when he spoke with a colleague about Ben's condition, he had referred to Ben as Danny.

"I quickly corrected myself," Robert said with a troubled frown. "But I wonder why I did that? Danny was my brother. He died seven years ago. And I realize now that ever since Ben told me about his illness, I can't get Danny out of my mind. But it doesn't make sense, because Danny didn't have cancer. He died in a sailing accident, and it was a long time ago."

The counselor asked about Danny. Robert was the oldest of six siblings, and Danny was the second. Robert said that he and Danny had been close and that Danny's death had devastated their family. He described his parents as so overwhelmed with shock and grief when Dan died that they didn't seem to be able to function. As the oldest child—none of his younger siblings lived in the same town, anyway—Robert took charge. He was the one who identified Danny's body, notified family members and friends, and made the arrangements for services and burial.

Discussing this with the counselor helped Robert see that he had been so busy with the arrangements and so focused on being strong to help his parents and others that he had avoided looking at his own grief and had never really mourned for Danny.

Robert left the EAP counselor's office with practical advice and information about how to manage the situation of an employee with a serious illness. Much of this, as he realized later, he already knew but hadn't been able to focus on. He also left with some insight into his own unresolved grief and a referral to a grief counselor.

Three sessions with a grief counselor helped Robert work through much of his grief about his brother. He was able to support and supervise Ben and his coworker, while continuing to manage the department's workload with more comfort and skill than he ever expected. Later he commented on how he felt that the grief counseling had helped him as a manager and as a person.

"One thing we talked about in counseling was the amount of energy I had spent avoiding my grief about Danny. But grief is everywhere, in everyone's life, so how can we avoid it? It seems to make it easier to just acknowledge this. I find myself more comfortable and helpful now when people are distressed—at home, with friends, and at work."

Others' Responses

Our society is often not helpful when we are working on this second task. From our immediate and extended families, our colleagues at work, our community, and the media, we may receive overt and covert messages about the need for us to be strong and to conceal any signs of our grief, at least in public. We may feel we have to hide our grief from others, that we have to protect them from our pain. We may feel a great deal of pressure to show others that we are coping, that we're handling our grief well, that we're getting over it.

Many people seem to reinforce our own understandable reluctance to face our grief. Some may try to distract us from our pain or seem to minimize what we are going through. They may tell us to remember the good times, not to keep thinking about the death or dwelling on the sadness. They may tell us to be strong, not to cry, or that it's time we got over it. They may say that the one who died wouldn't want us to be sad, that she or he would want us to go on with life.

Because these messages all seem to imply that we shouldn't have any pain, or at least that we shouldn't express any, we may try to numb our feelings, especially with alcohol or other drugs. In some of our ethnic groups and traditions, alcohol is a commonly offered remedy to grief. Medicines that help one sleep or that relieve anxiety may be offered to those who are grieving. The alcohol and other drugs are, at best, short-term solutions only, and when they wear off, the pain will still be there. By using alcohol and other drugs, we may even prolong the period of grieving, and we may also find that the alcohol and other drugs have become a problem.

Help That Hurts

Sometimes, in an attempt to comfort us when we are grieving, people say things that make our pain worse. Those who have had a child die may experience someone saying, "Well, at least you have other children." No matter how many other children you have, and how much you love them, the fact that you have them won't make up for a child's death.

A person whose spouse dies may hear someone say, "But, you're young, you'll marry again." This sounds very casual, as if you could just replace the person and the marriage.

When an older person dies, we may ask, "How old was she?" Survivors may feel we are suggesting that the person's advanced age makes the death easier or less significant.

Sometimes you may be told that a person's death will make you a better person, or that this death is part of God's plan.

People probably don't say these things to be hurtful; rather, they say them because they know you're hurting and want to help you feel better, or even because when you're sad it upsets them also. But even well-meant comments can hurt. You may feel hurt, resentful, or angry that the person making the comment seems to be minimizing your loss or trying to make you stop talking about it.

Sometimes you may brush off hurtful comments and think, "He means well." Other times you may become very upset, accuse people of being insensitive, yell at them that they don't know what they're talking about, or avoid any further contact.

Because these comments that hurt are so common, it can be helpful to consider how to respond in a way that lets people know what you want. You can say simply, "I know you're trying to make me feel better, but right now I need to feel sad." You could even add, "Having these feelings now is helping me complete the tasks of grieving so I can heal."

Several years after his son's suicide, Frank attended a presentation at his church on helping people who are grieving. Later he told his pastor that the priest who had been at the church when his son died should have had some training in grief counseling. When the pastor asked why, he said, "The person tonight said people who are grieving need someone to listen to their story and their sadness—it's more helpful than trying to give advice or explanations about what happened."

Frank described feeling distraught because his son was dead, and distressed and very troubled because he had killed himself. He had turned to the church, hoping to find some comfort or peace. He went on to say that the previous pastor had stopped him from talking about his son's death, telling him he'd already heard what had happened. He told Frank that instead of talking about the death, he should pray for understanding of God's will.

"At that point I couldn't pray, I couldn't even think straight. I kept picturing what he might have been feeling or thinking to have been so desperate, and I was in anguish. I went to the church wanting someone to recognize my pain and be with me, and I left feeling angry and abandoned. They say that God never abandons us, but some of the people who claim to speak for God certainly do."

Who Can Help

Often the most valuable person for us when we're grieving is one who gives us permission not to be strong, who understands that we're sad, or that we don't feel like being sociable, or that we need to cry. It can be especially helpful when someone says, "If you feel like talking about his death, know that I'm willing to listen."

It may be particularly helpful if that person reminds us that painful feelings are to be expected when we grieve and that experiencing them helps us go through our grief toward healing. If we see these reactions in the context of working on the tasks of grieving, then it's easier to see that we need to feel sad, or lonely, or angry, and that we may need to cry and talk about how unhappy we are.

Points to Remember

- Grief hurts.
- Experiencing the pain is the second task of grieving.
- Going through the pain can help us find peace and healing from our grief.
- Some well-meaning people can make you feel worse. If possible, avoid those who tell you what you "should" think or feel.
- Usually the people who are most helpful are those who respect your feelings and reactions and are willing to just be with you, however you're doing.
- Going on with life is easier if we take time to grieve.

Chapter 7

Living Without
the One Who Died

Dear Bron,

We're so glad you came to visit us, although the time went so quickly. Maybe next time you'll stay longer than a week. And thank you for helping Craig and me celebrate our birthdays. The rosebushes you gave us are lovely and seem to be thriving.

I smile when I remember our teasing you about birthday cards. You and Elizabeth always sent great cards, but we all knew who picked them out—and it wasn't you! Since Elizabeth's death, most of the family has wondered if we'd ever receive a card from you again! We all knew Elizabeth's enthusiasm for cards. Remember how we all teased her the time she gave you seven anniversary cards because "the words were just right"?

Elizabeth spent the time and energy to find cards that were "just right" for both the recipient and the occasion, and we all miss these very tangible signs of her thoughtfulness. Like the rest of us, you will miss receiving the cards she gave you.

Unlike the rest of us, you will also miss the cards she

used to find for family birthdays, your parents' anniversary, and the achievements of colleagues. Now you have to take over this role, or it won't get done.

This is what the third task of grieving is about: learning to live without the person who died. This seems obvious—that's what you're doing. You miss Elizabeth and you're adjusting to living without her. What is also happening is that in addition to missing her, you also miss all the different roles she played in your life—everything she did for you and with you.

The role of picking out cards is a simple example. You will find that there are many, many roles she played in your life—as wife, friend, lover, business partner—and some of those roles you may not have noticed while she was alive. So this third task involves having to figure out the gaps left in your life because Elizabeth isn't there anymore, as well as how to take care of some of the roles that used to be hers.

It will probably be a major task to learn to live without her. You may feel that when Elizabeth died, so did part of you. Some of the roles Elizabeth played will never be filled.

An even more important part of this third task is to recognize the significance of your relationship. This is so crucial for healing that I'm leaving it until next time so we can consider this separately.

I'm enclosing some information about hospice programs in your area, in case you want to find a grief group. It's almost four months since Elizabeth died, and this is often the toughest time. Also, the four-month anniversary of her death falls the day before her birthday, which may make it worse. I'm not saying don't be sad—you probably will be. A grief group could offer some support in your sadness.

Whatever you do, remember we love you. Craig and I and the children talk about you and how you're doing. We all enjoyed your visit; please come again whenever you can.

Love,

THE third task of grieving is learning to live without the one who died. This seems obvious—that's what we do when people we love die—we miss them and we learn to live without them. However, even if it's obvious, it is rarely simple or easy.

In addition to missing individuals, we also miss all the different roles they played in our lives—everything they did for us and with us. Many of the roles will be easy to identify, others may be more obscure. Working to complete this third task involves identifying those roles and the gaps now left in our lives. Then we need to find ways to fill in those gaps.

Variety of Roles

The amount of work associated with this third task can vary depending upon the number and type of roles played in your life by the person who died. Generally, if he played many roles in your life, it will take more work to adjust to living without him.

If you join a new company and a colleague dies a month later, that person may have played no role in your life. But if the one who died had oriented you to your responsibilities, she might have had many roles in your life in that month. She might have been your mentor, support person, and the one who explained the boss's idiosyncrasies. Maybe she warned you about the office gossip and showed you the best local lunch spots.

The roles played by a loving, involved, ever-present parent of a young child can be quite different from those of an elderly, failing parent who isn't always sure who you are. A cousin who lives nearby, helps with your child care crises, and shares with you the organization of family gatherings may have many important roles in your life. A sibling who lives far away, visits every few years, and calls only on holidays may have few.

Learning to live without a spouse or partner who died can be particularly difficult. Being a couple often means doing many things for each other, and most couples divide up roles and responsibilities. Sometimes we do this consciously: "You take care of the car, I'll take charge of the checkbook; I'll go to work, you stay home with the children."

Often we develop patterns of behavior in less deliberate ways, maybe without much thought or discussion. One person makes coffee in the morning, the other lets out the cat and brings in the newspaper. One person cooks dinner, the other cleans up the kitchen. One picks up where the other leaves off.

Sometimes we take turns playing particular roles, but often we find that one person usually does a particular task. So when that person isn't there anymore that task doesn't get done: we run out of bread, we can't find a health insurance form, the taxes aren't filed, we don't know what to cook for dinner or how to change the oil in the car.

Each time you realize that something didn't happen because the person who died always took care of it, you're reminded of the death and your loss. Thinking about this may help you understand why you seem to overreact at times when you're grieving.

Eva was seen by her family and friends as a very strong, capable person. When her husband died, the general opinion was that if anyone could handle two small children and a full-time job, she could. And she did seem to be managing, although not surprisingly she always looked tired, and many mornings when she went to work after dropping the children off, her eyes were puffy from crying the night before.

Then one evening her friend dropped in and found Eva sitting on the floor, crying so hard her friend could hardly understand what she was saying. Eva sobbed that she had settled the children to sleep, come into the kitchen to clean up their dinner dishes, and as she picked up the bag of garbage to take it outside, it broke open and spilled on the floor.

"I feel so silly to be crying because Raoul isn't here to take out the garbage! I miss him in so many ways, all of them much more important than that."

The garbage wasn't really the issue; rather, the fact that it hadn't been taken out reminded Eva why her husband wasn't there to do that chore—he was dead. When the garbage bag broke, her first reaction was to be angry with him.

"This was always your job, Raoul. Why did you leave me with so much to do? It's not fair!"

Because Eva was a strong, capable woman, she, and others, never doubted her ability to manage after her husband's death. But being able to manage does not mean that there is no pain. Taking over roles that had been his reinforced for her the pain of the empty spaces his loss left in her life and heart.

You may find that simple tasks that are left undone may precipitate apparently disproportionate amounts of tears and sadness. Your reaction may seem out of proportion if you think it was caused by the task that wasn't done, but not if you realize it was caused by the circumstance—the death—that led to the task not being done.

What You Need to Do

Having figured out the gaps left in your life because the person who died is no longer in his familiar roles, you need to determine how you're going to manage.

Some of this may be easy because you know how to do a specific task, and your biggest difficulty may be handling the emotions associated with taking over this role. Perhaps he always did the grocery shopping because his schedule was flexible and he could go when the store was less busy. But you know how to plan menus and shop for a week's meals, so you take over this task.

Other tasks you may not take over directly, but you can find a workable solution. Perhaps she used to take the car in when it needed service because she could catch a bus from the garage to work, but no bus runs anywhere near your job. Maybe now you and a coworker arrange to meet at the garage when either of you needs to take your car in—helping each other with this task.

It can be stressful for a newly widowed woman to pay bills and balance the checkbook because "he always took care of our finances." It can be equally stressful for a newly widowed man to learn to cook because "my wife always did the cooking."

Although these examples may sound like stereotypes, they are common issues for many people. For others there may be fewer roles that had been assumed because of gender, but there will still be roles that were assumed because of individual preference.

The fact that a task seems simple does not necessarily indicate that it won't be stressful to learn. It can be hard to make changes even when we want to. It is even worse when we wish we didn't have to and in fact hate the circumstances that require us to change.

What if there is a role or task you have never done, have no interest in or talent for, or are just not able to learn? Then you need to figure out other ways of handling it. An older woman who has never driven and whose husband of fifty years just died may not want or even be able to learn to drive. Perhaps she can learn the times and the routes of the bus system. Maybe she can arrange for lifts from neighbors to the store, library, or church, or can budget for a couple of cab rides a week.

Some Roles Cannot Be Filled

When someone important to you dies, you may feel that a part of you has died too, leaving big, empty spaces in your life. Some of the roles she or he played will never be filled, and this brings you back to the first and second tasks. Noticing the empty spaces and realizing that the person you love will not return to fill them can help you believe the death is real and make you face the pain that is the way to healing. All of these tasks relate to one another, and really we work on them all together.

The part of this third task that can be most difficult is learning to live without the relationship you shared, particularly if it was a close, loving, supportive relationship. We'll consider this aspect of living without someone in the next chapter.

Points to Remember

- The third task of grieving is learning to live without the one who died.
- We miss both the presence of the one who died and the roles which she or he played in our lives.

73

- We need to identify those roles and their significance.
- Apparently disproportionate reactions when simple tasks are left undone may be related to the fact of the death, rather than the task.
- Adjusting to new roles can be difficult.
- Other people can help us figure out different ways to manage.
- Some roles will never be filled.

Chapter 8

New Relationships

Dear Bron,

Should I be feeling guilty because it's been a while since I wrote? My excuse is that we talked so much when you were here with us, but actually that's been a while now, hasn't it? Anyway, I'm sending you lots of apologies, and even some guilt—I'm always good at guilt!

Today I want to talk more about the third task, but please don't feel pressured because you haven't completed the others yet. There's no "correct" schedule or sequence to this process—you'll probably be working on each of the tasks at different times, or at the same time, for many more months.

The third task is learning to live without Elizabeth. You're doing this by considering all the roles she played in your life and trying to find other ways to fill those roles. Part of this task—for all of us—is considering the part she played in our relationships. If we understand and grieve for the relationship we had with her, we'll be better able to develop new relationships. This doesn't mean that in order to heal from the grief of Elizabeth's death Karen will need a new mother, Lynn a new daughter, or you a new wife. The relationship each of you had with Elizabeth is unique and can't be replaced.

You loved Elizabeth when she was alive, and you'll continue to love her after her death, but gradually there will be some changes. This doesn't mean you don't love her anymore, or that you're starting to forget her. You'll find that you begin to transfer some of your emotional energy away from your relationship with Elizabeth and move toward investing that energy into others. They may be relationships with people who are new in your life, or established relationships may change, perhaps becoming closer or taking on new meaning.

Please be cautious when friends think that the way to help you through your grief is to "fix you up" with someone new. When we're grieving we're usually lonely and vulnerable. A new relationship may offer comfort and distraction. But the grief is still there and the mourning still needs to happen. If you don't grieve now, it will resurface another time.

Let me know what you think about all this.

Love,

THE third task of grieving is learning to live without the person who died. Some aspects of this we discussed in the last chapter. In this chapter we'll focus particularly on learning to live without the relationship you shared.

Recognize the Changes

The relationship you had with the one who died, and your love for each other, was unique. After the death, you'll continue to love the person, but gradually the relationship will begin to change. You will grieve for the relationship you have lost, although in many ways that relationship is never lost.

Usually when someone you love dies, you constantly feel full of emotions, and those emotions are usually very strong. You may feel *very* sad, *very* angry, *very* lonely, and the feelings may be so strong that you feel them physically. Over time, these feelings may diminish in intensity and frequency. Rather than an excruciating pain of loneliness, you'll feel a milder ache. Rather than being furious that she died and left you, you'll feel regret. Rather than feeling abandoned as the only person left in the world, you're lonely for the special times you used to share.

Sometimes it isn't the intensity of the pain that diminishes, but the frequency with which you feel it. The pain of losing the person you love may be as severe as ever, but you feel that pain less often.

Some people find these changes disturbing because they interpret them as meaning that they are forgetting the person who died or are ceasing to love him. But what these signs mean is that the relationship is changing, that instinctively you are withdrawing some emotional energy from the relationship.

Reinvesting

Your relationship with the person who died was a source of emotional nurturing for you. After the death you miss that nurturing, love, support, closeness, and the presence of a well-loved person in your life. However, you still need such nurturing and eventually you'll probably find yourself seeking it through new relationships or by deepening present relationships.

This does not mean that you should, or could, replace the deceased spouse, parent, child, or friend. Many of us know, or at least have heard of, someone who tried replacing a spouse almost immediately after the death—often with disastrous results. Because each person is unique, each relationship is different. It is not possible to replace an individual or a relationship. People who are grieving usually are lonely and vulnerable, and a new relationship may offer comfort and distraction. But the grief is still there and the mourning still needs to happen. When the grief surfaces later it can lead to difficult complications in the new relationship.

Well-meaning friends may try to help you find someone new to take your mind off your sadness.

Ira said he would never marry again. He said it many times during his wife's final illness and in the months that followed her death. Some friends recognized the extent of his sadness and tried to respect his privacy; others saw his loneliness as a challenge and were determined to find someone special to help him "get over his loss."

If it hadn't been so sad, it would have been funny to hear friends tell very similar stories about their attempts to "help."

"We invited Ira and several other people for dinner the other night. I wanted Ira to meet Sally, a friend of ours who is such a lovely person. Ira ignored her completely! When they were introduced, he just nodded and didn't say anything at all. He made no attempt to talk with her all evening, and even moved away from a discussion he was having with the Smiths when she joined in. I had him sit next to her at dinner, and he gradually turned his whole body away until he was sitting with his back to her! It was unbelievable!"

Some of the friends thought Ira had been very rude, because after all they had "only been trying to help," and Ira could at least have been polite. Ira's view was that he had said no to many offers to meet women, that it was rude of others to discount what he had said, and ignoring Sally was the only way they might realize he meant what he said. Ira thought his friends were suggesting a substitute relationship, and he knew he hadn't finished grieving and didn't want a substitute.

The purpose of grieving is not to forget the person who died, or to diminish the importance of your relationship. Rather, it is to find healing of most of the pain of your loss.

Not Completing This Task

Sometimes people do not complete this task of learning to live without the one who died. When a couple have shared many, many years in a loving, fun, satisfying marriage, the death of one partner may be followed closely by the death of the other. There may not seem to be any physical reason why the second person should deteriorate and die so quickly. Maybe she or he was unable—or unwilling—to learn to live without the other.

Suicide may also indicate that a survivor was not able to learn to live without the one who died. And sometimes the survivor doesn't die but seems to stop living. The physical body is still alive, but emotionally, socially, and spiritually, the person seems to be frozen.

Summary of the Tasks of Grieving

When you are grieving you may feel disturbed and confused by a swirl of emotions and a variety of reactions, many of which may not seem rational. These emotions and reactions take a toll. You may feel emotionally drained and physically exhausted by the work of grieving and mourning.

Identifying the specific tasks you need to work on will not make the process easy; the emotional pain will still hurt and your spiritual and existential questions will continue. Understanding the tasks of grieving can help on an intellectual level, serving as a map or a guide to help you make sense of what you're going through. Your head and your heart may feel as if they are operating separately for a while, but eventually they will come together again.

The work is hard, although the tasks may sound rather simple. To work through your grief you have to:

1. Believe the death really happened.
2. Go through the pain of your grief.
3. Learn to live without the one who died.

In the last few chapters, we have considered each task separately, to help you understand the work you need to do and realize what might help you find some healing from your grief. Mostly you won't work on each task by itself—many of the experiences you have will relate to two or more tasks. The first and second tasks are closely connected: the more you believe the death is real, the more it hurts; the more it hurts, the more you believe. The third task, learning to live without the person who died, can also be understood as learning to go on with life. To complete the third task we need to identify the roles that person played and find other ways to fill the gaps left by her/his death. We also need to recognize the significance of the relationship we shared and grieve our loss of that relationship.

It can also be helpful to consider the tasks along with the stages of grief. The stages are disbelief, pain, and healing. In the first stage we work mainly on the first task, believing the death is real. In the second stage we work mainly on the second task, going through our grief, and in the third stage we work mainly on the third task, learning to live without the person. The tasks correspond to the stages of grieving.

This is a simple explanation of a very complex process. The explanation is not to try to minimize your pain, confusion, and distress. Rather it is to help you find some focus during a time that is often very bewildering. Trying to focus on a simple road map may help you find some direction, some pattern, and even some control of what is happening to you as you grieve.

Points to Remember

- It isn't possible to replace a person who died or the relationship you shared.
- Your relationship was a source of emotional nurturing, and you still need such nurturing.
- Although your relationship with the person who died will change, it doesn't mean you're forgetting him or her.
- Some emotional energy from that relationship can be reinvested in other relationships.
- The feelings of grief may decrease in intensity or frequency, and sometimes both.

Chapter 9

Why We Grieve Differently

Dear Bron,

I was interested in your comments about how other people seem to be handling Elizabeth's death. You're right, we're each in a different place with it, grieving in our own ways.

The major influences on how we each grieve Elizabeth's death are our various relationships with her, how we feel about the circumstances of her death, our past experiences, and our present situations.

Your experience as Elizabeth's husband is different from Lynn's as her mother, Karen's as her daughter, or mine as her friend. And there are differences for all other family members and friends. Because our relationships with Elizabeth were different, we can expect our grief to be different. Just as no one can ever really understand a relationship that others share, so no one can ever really understand another's grief.

I wonder how you feel about the circumstances of Elizabeth's death? For me, some of the circumstances are extremely distressing, for example, her age and her illness. I think fifty-two is much too young to die, and her dying of breast cancer brings back sadness about other friends who have died of this disease and stirs up my own fears. But some of the circumstances are not distressing to me and even feel comforting. Her death was peaceful and she did not suffer. She died at home, and we followed her wishes right to the end. We talked about everything that was important. These circumstances help me feel somehow satisfied.

Previous experiences vary and present circumstances are also very different. No one can ever know who has the easiest or the most difficult circumstances. My theory about this is that no matter what anyone else has to deal with, the worst possible pain is whatever I am feeling at this moment.

I have a friend, a very wise grief counselor, who says one of the most important ways to survive grief is to determine what your stance will be. She's seen many people make what turn out to be self-fulfilling prophecies, for example, "I'll never love again," or, "I'll never get over this."

To some extent the realization of the fact that we don't forget a person or that we don't get over the death is fine, but we also need to think about how we can heal. We might say, "This will be the hardest thing I've ever done, but I will get through it in time." Or, "I know I'm going to have some very sad, lonely times without her, but eventually it will be easier."

What's your stance? Let's talk about this.

Love,

IF everyone grieved in the same way, it would be easier to know what to expect when you grieve. But no one can give you a very clear picture, because there is no one way to grieve—grief is as individual as the people who grieve. What happens to you will be somewhat different from what happens to another.

One aspect of grieving that everyone has in common is that we all must go through it. That is true in two senses. First, that grief is a part of everyone's life, we all experience it; and second, we have to work through our grief, we cannot avoid it.

(Even with this aspect of grief there is an exception. If we experience multiple and continuing losses, working through each grief cannot happen in the same way.)

How you grieve, and how long and how difficult the grieving period is, depends upon many factors, including your relationship with the person who died, the circumstances of the death, your previous experiences with grief, and your present situation.

Your Relationship

Your relationship with the person who died will affect both the intensity and the duration of your grief. When the person was someone very close you'll expect more grief, and when you were not close you'll expect less.

You'll grieve more for your spouse or partner than for a casual acquaintance. The grief you experience when a friend with whom you have a close interdependent relationship dies is more painful than when the relationship is a casual one.

Some of the most difficult grief seems to be when the relationship was characterized by mixed feelings. This might happen if the person who died is a spouse with whom you've shared a very unsettled marriage, or a parent with whom you'd always had a strained relationship.

Carol's father had left the family when she was eleven. She and her brother, who was two years older, had decided that it would have been better if he'd left long before that. With their pain and anger just below the surface, they joked about his having given them "dysfunctional genes." His alcoholism and violent outbursts had scared and scarred them as small children. As teenagers they both began to struggle with their own problems with drinking. When they were in their twenties, both now sober and in recovery programs, their father died.

Carol refused to go to his funeral and thought her mother and brother were "stupid hypocrites" for attending. She cut off contact with them, saying she wanted nothing to do with them until they stopped this foolishness of pretending that her father's death was anything but a great relief.

She started drinking again, then added other drugs, and after several terrible weeks had to be hospitalized. During her time in the hospital, while seeing the counselor she was referred to, and in the recovery group to which she returned, she claimed she started drinking again because of her brother's "stupidity." She would, and still does, several years later, get angry with anyone who suggests her bout of heavy drinking might have been related to her father's death. Carol is still sober and still in recovery. Her father is rarely mentioned in her presence, and when he is, she flushes, her eyes narrow, and she insists upon changing the subject or leaves the room.

Those who know her feel that Carol has a lot of emotional pain and grief. Her grief may be connected to the death of her father, but probably she is not grieving a relationship she lost so much as a relationship she never had. Often people who have had a difficult or nonexistent relationship with a parent harbor a dream that one day that parent will change and their relationship will be wonderful.

In this kind of situation, when the parent dies, the children, even if they are now adults, may feel pain and anger associated with what they remember. The death also means an end to any belief that a nurturing relationship *might* develop. Instead of, or in addition to grieving the person, they may grieve for what they never had.

Previous Experience

Your earlier experiences with loss can influence how you deal with your present grief. What losses have you experienced? How did people support you through those losses? What did people tell you about loss and grief? What role models did you have? Did people model how to reach out to friends and families to both give and gain support and comfort? Did you learn that although grieving is painful and causes tears and sadness, you can survive and heal and it won't destroy you?

Did you learn not to talk about your sadness, that it was forbidden to cry, and that you should hide your grief? Were you scared because you thought no one else felt the pain you did, no one else shed the tears you did, no one else wanted to scream in anger at this death as you did? Did you fear that allowing yourself to express your pain would cause you to be overwhelmed by it, or that your pain might frighten others?

These early experiences influence your reactions now. If your early memories of death and grief are of a quietly sad family, talking in hushed voices, with all the curtains in the house closed, it may make you very uncomfortable to enter a home where grief is expressed through loud wailing and floods of tears. Your memories of services may be of lengthy rituals with music, prayer, readings, flowers, following the coffin to the graveyard, and another service at the graveside. Attending a brief, simple service, perhaps with a small urn of ashes rather than a body in a coffin, or no service at all, may leave you feeling very unsatisfied.

•

A person who was taught that crying is a sign of weakness may still need to cry and may still cry. But if the tears come in public, this person will also feel discomfort at behaving in a way she or he believes is inappropriate. Someone who was taught, probably by example rather than in words, that loud crying is how you show grief may feel that one who doesn't cry is "cold and unfeeling" or "didn't really love him" or may even "be glad she died."

When George retired at sixty-five, he and his wife, May, settled into a new routine together. This meant some adjustments, as May had not worked outside the home since their marriage and had always managed most of the household chores. Gradually George took over some tasks, and other chores they enjoyed doing together.

When George was sixty-seven, May died suddenly of a heart attack. May's death was extremely difficult for George. He missed her and suddenly felt much older. Their five children visited him often, and one daughter, Joyce, urged him to sell the home and move in with her family. George refused, but said he'd appreciate some help with cooking and managing the house, "just for a while, until I learn how to do all of this."

They set up a routine where Joyce helped George plan menus and develop grocery lists, and would come by and help him prepare some meals. She and her siblings agreed that although Dad was very quiet, he seemed to be coping quite well.

George attended a session on grief at the senior center, but left about halfway through. The next day he phoned the church office for an appointment with the minister. When George arrived, the minister ushered him into her office.

"How are you doing, George?" she said.

George struggled to speak, but before he could even say a word, he started to cry. He tried to apologize for his tears, and the minister assured him there was no need to apologize.

George tried to explain how sad and lost he felt and cried harder. He tried to stop crying and couldn't.

George and the minister met regularly for a few months, and at first George cried almost the whole time. Gradually he cried less, and they spoke more—of May, his sadness and loneliness since her death, how his life had changed, and how his family was doing.

George often apologized to the minister for his tears, and sometimes seemed embarrassed, but it was only during those sessions that he cried. Some of George's loneliness was because he was avoiding people for fear he might cry in their presence, which would be embarrassing to him.

Circumstances of the Death

The circumstances surrounding the death can greatly affect your grief. The death of an older person who lived a long, full life can somehow feel logical, no matter how saddened you are by your loss. The death of your child can be unbelievably difficult, can seem unbearable, and may *never* make sense to you.

A sudden death leads to a different grief from that following an expected death. Death from natural causes leads to grief different from the grief following a death in a car crash. Knowing the person died peacefully feels different from knowing she suffered. Any violence associated with a death, as when someone dies in wartime or is murdered, can add horror to our grief. Suicide adds extra pain, often regret or guilt that perhaps we might have done more, and anger that he *chose* to leave us.

Grief is certainly more complicated if the death could have been avoided, if there was an unresolved issue between you and the one who died, or if your main role in life was taking care of him or her.

Present Circumstances

Your personality and the ways you usually cope with stress in your life will affect how you grieve. Your age, financial status, gender, religious beliefs, country of origin, and ethnic and cultural background can all make a difference in your grieving.

If you're older, you may have confidence that no matter how bad your grief, you can survive it and even grow from it as you have with previous losses you have experienced. Or you may despair, wondering if there's anything left in life. When an older person's mate dies, ending a partnership of perhaps several decades, the surviving partner may also die, sometimes within weeks or a few months. For this person, under these circumstances, the stages and tasks of grieving may seem irrelevant. She or he may feel that learning to live without the person who died is not worth the effort, and any healing from their grief will come only in death.

Being younger may mean having less experience with death and more anxiety about how to go on with life. It may also mean greater flexibility in handling changed circumstances and greater resilience when faced with loss. In children, understanding of loss and expression of the grief can vary greatly, and often the most important factor to consider is the age of the child. (We'll address children's grief further in the next chapter.)

If the person who died provided your financial support, you may be anxious about the future or resentful that you and she didn't plan ahead better. With this death you lost a person, income and security, and maybe your home and possessions.

Gender is another factor that may affect grief. As always, we need to be wary of sweeping generalizations about gender differences. The differences between the grief of two men, or of two women, may be as great as those between men and women generally.

Grief—the internal feelings associated with loss—is probably very similar in men and women. However, mourning—the outward expression of the pain of our loss—may seem quite different. This may be more because of what we were taught about socially acceptable behaviors for each gender than because of any intrinsic difference.

Women's styles of grieving and mourning often reflect their focus on relationships. They are often able to express pain openly, and accept and utilize emotional support and practical assistance. Men's styles are more likely to focus on action. They want to find out what's happening to them, and how they can use their strengths to take action to deal with this pain.

As with any other difference that seems to be related to gender, it can be helpful to explore which of your reactions and behaviors are more typically female or male responses to grief. Most of us are an interesting mix, and we can certainly benefit from exploring what we can learn from another style.

Men have often been socialized in ways that affect their grieving. Many boys and young men are taught that tears are for babies, that crying is a sign of weakness, and that men have to be strong. Like George, whom we mentioned earlier, some men are embarrassed and apologetic if anyone sees them cry and try to keep a very tight rein on their emotions for fear that any display of their grief will be thought unmanly.

Although it is not uncommon to find women who struggle with similar concerns about outward displays of grief, this seems to be more of a problem for men. Generally speaking, our society is more accepting of women's tears than men's.

Men may find their own difficulties with expressing grief are compounded by overt and covert messages from others.

Keith, whose young child had died, commented on the number of people who asked him how his wife was doing, but not how *he* was. He felt the implication was that death may not be as distressing to a man as to a woman, or that a man is better at "handling" his grief than a woman is.

Although this may have been the implication, sometimes people find it easier to ask about someone else rather than the person to whom they are speaking. Very often parents will find that people ask them how the children (of any age) are handling things. Or children (of any age) may be asked how a parent is managing.

It's very important not to make assumptions about the influence of any one factor, such as age, gender, and particularly religious beliefs and ethnic or cultural traditions.

Religious beliefs may be a source of great strength for you, cause you to feel guilt, or lead to family conflict. Religious rituals can be immensely comforting and significant, or they may seem irritating and meaningless. Even within families whose members share apparently similar belief systems, there are often individual interpretations and influences.

The ways in which various ethnic and cultural traditions approach dying, death, and grief can be extremely interesting and very important. Often the influence of these traditions lingers, maybe unconsciously, in people who consider themselves far removed from their roots. They may move closer to their roots and to their cultural rituals at times of crisis, especially in times of sickness or death.

However, cultures change, traditions change, and people change. This is particularly important to remember in countries with many immigrants, such as the United States. If we assume that all Korean people deal with death one way, or all Polish people deal with death another way, we fail to appreciate the constant changes in life and culture. At the very least there may be differences in attitudes between first, second, or third generations of immigrants, and there are usually many more differences among individuals in those generations. The differences that develop and the changes that occur are usually not predictable. Most of us are products of numerous influences. It's sometimes difficult to understand one's own responses and usually impossible to know the influences affecting others.

Expectations

Many factors, including our relationships to the one who died, the circumstances of the death, our previous experiences with grief, and our present situation, can influence what we expect of ourselves and others when we grieve. Perhaps more important than our individual expectations is the congruence of the expectations of everyone involved. You may expect to cry loudly and be very emotional and let everyone else make decisions and arrangements, but be surrounded by those who expect you to be strong and take care of everything and everyone.

Tension and criticism can easily result when there are such differing expectations. People may feel that others don't know how to behave. One person may assume that the other isn't "upset enough" and therefore must be unaffected by the death, or one may assume the other is overreacting, being melodramatic, or making a fuss to gain attention.

It helps to be open about what you want when you're grieving, especially if others' needs seem different. You might say: "I've never been one to cry in public, so I need some private time for a little while." Or perhaps in a reverse situation: "I just can't stop the tears."

When we're grieving ourselves, it may be hard to understand why others react differently. But there is no *one* way to grieve, and each of us is an individual. We need to remember and respect differing styles of grief, and try not to judge harshly those who don't meet our expectations of grieving.

Points to Remember

- We all grieve differently.
- Many factors affect how individuals grieve.
- The circumstances of the death may affect how we work on the tasks of grieving.
- Our previous experiences and present situations can affect our grief.
- What we have learned about how we "should" grieve may not help, and may even hinder our grieving.
- Our expectations and assumptions of what is acceptable behavior when grieving may be quite different from those of other people.

Chapter 10

Helping Grieving Children

Dear Bron,

   Karen's comments about how the boys seem to be deal-
ing with Elizabeth's death certainly point out the differ-
ences in their ages and personalities. They are great
kids—I was very impressed with them during the last few
weeks Elizabeth was alive and during the services and
family gatherings. I'm enclosing some general informa-
tion about grieving children, and a couple of books.

   I find myself worrying a little about Karen. Sometimes,
and understandably, a parent seems to try to take care of
each child's pain before looking at her own. Karen is such
a loving person and such a great mom to the boys that I'm
sure she frequently puts their needs before her own.
Because of this, I wouldn't be surprised if Karen grieves
for a long time. Also, the relationship she and Elizabeth
had was so very close that I'm sure Karen misses her
mother a great deal.

   I'm glad you and Karen are able to support and comfort
each other. Take care of yourself and each other and those
great boys.

                                   Lots of love to you all,

CHILDREN experience loss and grief. When children lose something that is important to them—perhaps a favorite blanket or toy—they feel sad and upset and they cry. They're grieving. When they lose the presence in their lives of people they love, children grieve. They grieve because grief is a normal response to loss, and loss is a part of life from our very earliest days.

Children need support in their grief because grief hurts and because childhood is a time to learn skills they'll need in life. With support, children, especially young ones, often handle dying, death, and grief better than adults expect they will.

Common Concerns of Parents

For many parents and other adults, talking with children about death and grief is uncomfortable. Sometimes they avoid or delay any discussion of death because they think a child is too young to understand. They feel uncertain about what they should say or fear they may upset the child.

Instinctively, most parents try to protect children from anything that might hurt them. When they're little we keep tight hold of their hands when crossing streets, and when they're older we warn them of the dangers of tobacco and alcohol. We want to protect them from emotional pain as well as physical injury. We try to change things if our children are teased or bullied at school or if their friends turn against them.

This instinct to protect children can lead parents to try to shield children from the realities of death and grief. Because grief hurts we want to keep children away from it. This may lead us to replace the goldfish before the child realizes it's dead, or to say "Don't cry, we'll buy you another" if the child has lost or broken a favorite toy. Or perhaps to tell a child that a grand-father has gone on a long vacation, rather than that he died.

We may manage to replace the goldfish. If the replacement fish also dies, however, and so do any further replacements, we may get tired of the subterfuge. And we've missed a chance to help a child learn something about death.

When we soothe the pain of the lost toy with promises of a new one, we're teaching that grief can be eased with replace-ments. Sometimes we want children to do this—if they can't make the school team in basketball, maybe they can choose another sport. But do we want them to learn that when someone you love dies, you just find someone else?

A child told that a dead grandparent has gone away may have questions and concerns about why he left without saying good-bye. She may wonder why he wanted to leave her, when he will be back, or whether others will leave her also.

Children are not deceived by efforts to hide the truth about a death. They realize that someone has disappeared and that other people are upset. When what they're told doesn't seem congru-ent with the emotional distress they perceive, they may decide that whatever happened cannot be talked about, so it must be too terrible to discuss. They may also think this not believable explanation is a message to not ask questions.

Imagination can produce worse scenarios than the truth. When children sense sadness and pain and are given no expla-nation or one that seems inadequate, they may assume they are the cause of the distress. They may also feel excluded from the family and may wonder what they did to cause that. These pos-sibilities can be much more frightening for children than any reality.

How and when we talk about death with our children and what we say will depend on our own beliefs and experiences and on the age and experiences of the children. It will also depend upon the particular situation that prompted the discussion. Talking about a dead cat on the street is obviously quite different from a parent discussing the other parent's death.

Common Concerns for Children

Children respond to loss in different ways. The age of a child may help us determine where she or he is in her or his development. However, all children develop differently. We cannot assume all three-year-olds will have the same questions, that all five-year-olds will have the same fears, that all adolescents will have similar behavioral responses. Children are just as individual in their grief as those of us who are older. Considering common concerns of children of different ages can help us anticipate what might be an individual child's particular questions and needs.

Very Young Children

Many people assume that very young children cannot possibly understand if someone dies, but it is not unusual to see even babies become upset when there is a death in the family. Children under the age of two or three generally have no clear understanding of the reality of death. These very young children may not *understand,* but something has changed in their lives and they can *feel* a sense of loss.

All parents know that even when children are too young to talk they still are able to communicate their feelings. When someone dies, babies may become fretful and tearful or they may be reluctant to eat, smile, or play. They may be distressed by separation from someone they love, they may fear being abandoned, and they may react to the sadness of people around them.

At this age what children most need is familiarity and consistency. They usually are comforted by being cared for by those people who have always cared for them, with the same routine and in the same environment as usual. This isn't possible, however, if the one who died was a parent or regular caregiver, or if the parent or parents travel for the death and funeral.

These very young children need a little more attention than usual, perhaps extra cuddling when they cry or extra rocking to help them sleep. If there are changes in caregiving, it helps to establish a new routine or return to the old one as soon as is reasonable. We need to respond to the infant's feelings of distress by making her feel secure and loved.

Between Ages Three and Seven

Children in this age group understand that death happens—that people, animals, and plants die—but they are uncertain about what that means. They may see death as temporary. "Mommy died, but she'll be back soon."

They are old enough to talk about death and may ask lots of questions, the same way they question anything that comes to their attention. They're often very much interested in the physical details and may want to know what happens when someone dies or what it feels like to be dead. They may worry about what it's like for the one who died: "Won't Grandpa be cold now that he's buried under the ground?"

Generally what children in this age group need is to receive simple and clear answers to their questions and reassurance that they are loved and will be taken care of.

Between Ages Eight and Eleven

Children in this age group know that everyone dies, and they're learning what that means. They understand the concept of terminal illness, that death has causes, and that death is final and people who die don't come back to life.

Beginning to understand more about death may lead some children to be curious and want more details. Some may be scared by the idea of death and try to avoid thinking or talking about it. Others will alternate between some curiosity and some apprehension.

In these years they are beginning to deal with the possibility that they too may die. They may wonder what it would be like to die, but usually don't see their own deaths as a reality. As their lives expand in these years, and friends and peer groups become very important, their concerns and questions about death extend beyond themselves. They are more aware of a community's issues about coping with death and grief.

In addition to reassurance of love, children in these years need opportunities for reading, discussions, and reflection to explore their understanding of life and death.

Ages Twelve and Over

Teenagers think about death. They may be fascinated by poetry, books, and movies (including horror movies) that deal with death. By now they may have had to face major losses, perhaps the death of a relative, a friend, or a pet. If they haven't, they probably will during these years. In addition to deaths of older people whom they know, they may experience the deaths of people in public life, in their neighborhood, or perhaps the death of a teacher or a peer.

As the realization of their mortality develops, it may produce extreme anxiety. Attempting to cope with this anxiety can lead to the risk-taking behavior that is not uncommon in this age group.

For many young people, these can be turbulent years. There are many changes and a great deal to be learned for those moving into adulthood. The death of someone they love can be devastating, especially if they have not already learned how to cope, at least somewhat, with grief.

Like anyone else, teenagers need loving support and understanding when they grieve. In these years they're trying to define themselves more clearly, and may seem to vacillate between the children they were and the adults they're becoming. They may struggle between dependence and independence in the family. Their peers are important to them and peer relationships can be a great source of support. However, the need to belong to that peer group can lead to stress if they feel that their grief does not fit the norm for the group.

•

Whatever their ages, all children dealing with loss and grief need information, reassurance that they are loved and will be taken care of, and help in finding ways to express and manage their grief. Their needs are similar to those of many adults.

How to Help: Communicate

Give information. Children of all ages need to know what happened. The information we give them needs to be *age appropriate,* which means appropriate to their level of understanding. A twelve-year-old may understand: "All of Grandma's medicines weren't able to control her high blood pressure any longer. Last night, she had a stroke and died." A four-year-old may understand, "Grandma has not been well for a long time, and last night she got very sick. She was so sick she couldn't get better and she died."

Don't overwhelm a child with too much detail and too many explanations. It's usually easier to give a brief answer and then see if he has another question. Often children will think over what you have said and come back later with further questions.

Use language that is as *simple and clear* as possible. Don't be afraid to use words such as "death" or "dead." They may seem blunt to you, but they are more easily understood than euphemisms, which can lead to misunderstandings with serious consequences. If the disappearance of someone a child loved is explained as "he went to sleep" and everyone is crying and upset, the child may develop problems going to sleep. Or if we tell a child: "He was so good that God took him to live in Heaven," we shouldn't be surprised if the child tries very hard never to be good again, in case God decides she too should have to go away.

For many people, religion is a major source of comfort and strength when they're facing death—their own or another's. If religion is an important part of your life and your family, it helps you teach your children about death.

Catherine was five when her father died. A week later she explained to a visiting friend of her mother's that "Daddy's body is buried up—it's in the garden next to church. But the part of Daddy that loves me has gone to Heaven."

It may be a relief for children to know a beloved parent is now waiting for them in Heaven, and that we can be pleased that God is taking care of him. It may also be very confusing to them that we also feel intense grief and pain. It is important to share your beliefs with your children, and to share your sadness at losing the physical presence of someone you love. Catherine also said, "Sometimes me and Mommy miss Daddy so much we have to hug each other and cry."

If religion has not been part of a child's life, a sudden introduction of religious explanations may be confusing, and may need careful explanation and exploration with the child.

Listen. Explore the child's understanding of whatever she has been told. Don't assume that she heard what you said or that she understood it. Be prepared to answer the same questions several times.

Pay attention to the child's reaction. Is he tearful, puzzled, angry, or seemingly unaffected? What concerns does he voice? Is there more than he's saying? Being aware of some concerns common to children may help you better understand a question, so that you can help the child explore the concern.

Often children fear that they somehow caused the death, and feel guilty for their perceived responsibility for the death. "If I hadn't been naughty, Grandma wouldn't have died."

Children may worry that others, including themselves, may die. "Are you going to die too, Dad?" "Are we all going to be killed now, Mommy?"

Sometimes children can feel very angry because the person died and left them, and they feel abandoned. If parents or others who frequently take care of them die, they may worry about who will take care of them now.

Not all children will ask questions. Some children are more reticent, and some will think about things for a long time. Often children understand quickly that a parent is uncomfortable with a particular topic, and they won't ask questions. Don't assume that a child who doesn't talk about the death is not thinking about it. Try mentioning how you are feeling about it to give the child an opening.

Be affectionate. However your child seems to react, know that the death, grief, and sadness may cause anxiety. It's important to tell *and show* your child that you love him and will take care of him. When children are anxious or distressed, hugging and holding them can be very comforting to them—and often to the parent as well. Sometimes teenagers may pull away from our hugs and kisses, but it's important to offer them.

Include them. Tell them *what will happen now,* remembering that a change in routine may be upsetting for some children. "Mom and I aren't going to work for the rest of this week. All your aunts and uncles will be coming until after the funeral and probably lots of friends will come and visit for a while. It's going to be busy here for the next several days, and it may seem like the phone is always ringing."

Share *your feelings and reactions.* "I'm so sad that I don't seem to be able to stop crying. I can't imagine what it will be like not having him around."

"Uncle Joe was Daddy's favorite brother, so Daddy's crying because he'll miss him so much."

Ask their *opinion.* "Mom and I are talking about the music for Grandma's funeral service. What do you think would be good?"

Give them *tasks.* Feeling useful helps children see their value to the family. You might ask young children to draw a picture or print a letter to give to another grieving person. Older children can be given errands to run or asked to help with answering the door or the phone.

Include them in *decisions.* Many parents have questions about children visiting dying people, or going to funerals, or seeing the body, or kissing the dead person goodbye. Generally the best way to handle these concerns is to explain what will happen and ask the children how they want to participate.

Mary, her husband, and her three children were taking a vacation with her sister Jackie and her husband and their two children. Returning from an afternoon at the beach, they received a message that the sisters' mother, who was in a nursing home because of severe dementia, had had a stroke and was dying.

The parents explained to the children, who ranged in age

from six to twelve years, what had happened to their grand-mother. Then they talked about what should happen next.

"Aunt Jackie and I are going to be with Nana. We don't know when she'll die, maybe tonight or tomorrow or not for another few days. We want to talk about what you children want to do.

"Your aunt and I can go now and you can all stay here with Uncle Tom and Daddy. Or Daddy could come with us and you children could all stay here with Uncle Tom. Or we could all go to see Nana tonight and say goodbye, and then Daddy and Uncle Tom can bring you all back here tomorrow, while Aunt Jackie and I stay with Nana."

The children were concerned because of their mothers' sadness and had several questions. "What will Nana look like now?" "Did it hurt her to have a stroke?" "How long does it take to die?" "Aren't we going to have any dinner tonight?" "If you and Mom go now can't you come back here again in the morning?" "Does this mean the vacation's over? But it's only Monday—you said we'd stay until Saturday!" "Can I go and pick some flowers for Nana?"

The children also expressed some opinions, and they didn't always agree. "I want to see Nana, but I don't want to watch the dying part." "We could pick all those pink roses in the garden." "I hope there won't be too many prayers." "I want to go to the beach again tomorrow." "Remember when the lady from school died and we all went home early?"

Tim, who was nine, struggled not to cry as he said, "I don't know what we should do but I think we should all stay together."

They all agreed on this. During the three-hour drive to the nursing home, there were more questions and more opinions. There were also some tears, some arguments, and some conversations completely unrelated to Nana or death.

They reached the nursing home about 10 P.M. All the family—adults and children—gathered around the bed and joined with the priest in prayer. The nurse in charge brought tea and cookies and they sat for a while at the bedside. The children seemed relieved when the adults suggested it was past bedtime and that their fathers would take them home while their mothers stayed with Nana. None of the children wanted to kiss their grandmother goodbye, though they each touched her hand and said, "Good night, God bless, Nana," as they left the room. Their grandmother died early the next morning.

Like many adults, the children didn't know what they wanted to do; and they had lots of feelings and reactions. There was sadness for their grandmother, and because their mothers were upset. There was resentment because of the interruption to a long-anticipated vacation. There was fear of the unknown.

The adults gave the children time and opportunities to talk, think, cry, ask questions, complain, and participate. Also, they recognized that the children needed some time to be kids.

The fathers took the children swimming one morning while the mothers met with the priest to plan music and readings for the funeral. The children worked together making fruit salad and setting the table while one set of parents took a quiet walk together and the other parents cooked dinner.

The children visited the funeral home with their parents to say a little prayer by their grandmother's body. One of them said, "She looks sort of empty." Another disagreed, "She looks the same as usual, but she feels different." The six-year-old suggested they go for ice cream.

The day of the funeral they picked every flower in the garden for bouquets they carried to church and later placed on the grave. They were solemn and attentive during the service, joined in the prayers and hymns, and watched with interest as the coffin was lowered into the grave.

Later, during the meal at their aunt's house they gradually became less serious. Their good clothes looked less tidy and their voices became louder. Eventually they, their cousins, and the children of neighbors and friends drifted outside and began a marathon soccer match in the backyard.

Start early to teach about death. Children are learning all the time, and there are many opportunities to teach them gradually about death. It's much easier to talk about death with your child if he asks you about a caterpillar that was squashed on the sidewalk, than to start when his favorite uncle dies.

The eulogies and funerals your children organize for dead goldfish may seem tedious; you might prefer to simply flush the fish. The stories in which an animal dies may cause your child to cry and you to be concerned about his sadness. Your child's questions about death may make you admit you don't know all the answers, or stir up your own fears and discomfort concerning death.

How you respond to children always teaches them something. Participating in funerals for goldfish or other pets can offer opportunities to help children learn about death.

Reading together books that mention death can be an opportunity for more learning and more closeness. I'm sure that *Charlotte's Web* has provided many parents with a chance to talk about death with their children.

Sooner or later—certainly sooner than most of us expect—our children learn that we don't know everything. We can teach them another lesson when we admit what we don't know or what our discomforts may be.

Whatever we say to children, they really learn more from what we do.

Do they learn that when someone we love dies, we are sad and tearful, but are still able to function? Do they learn not to ask us about death because we avoid the topic, or do we become so distressed that they feel guilty for upsetting us?

Do they see us bake bread and take it when we go to visit a newly bereaved family? Do they see us avoid a neighbor whose wife died? Do they hear us judge others for the way they grieve? Do they hear us say it's hard to know what to say to someone grieving but then we try anyway?

Do we teach them that if they cry or tell us they're upset, we'll demand they pull themselves together? Do we show them that we don't forget those who have died, we miss their presence, and we enjoy our memories?

Do we teach them that we will tell them what to believe, what to do, how to feel, and that they're too young to question us? Do they learn that we are able to admit our own uncertainties, respect their opinions, and support their explorations?

Parents have the responsibility and the privilege to begin their children's learning about many things which will affect their lives. Learning about death, loss, and grief can be a lifelong process. We don't teach them, nor do they learn, in one lesson. However, we can help them construct a foundation for future learning.

What we teach our children about death will also teach them about life. What we demonstrate by our behavior with them when we are grieving will also teach them about relationships. We can teach them that life is not always easy, that relationships are precious, that we should treat others with respect, and how people who care about each other—families, friends, and communities—can love and support one another during crises.

Points to Remember

- Children grieve.
- Even before children understand about death intellectually, they respond to it emotionally.

- Children need simple information, and opportunities to clarify what they've heard.
- Attempts to avoid talking with children about death, or to deceive them about a specific death, lead to more anxiety and distress than the truth.
- Children need reassurance that they are loved and will be taken care of.
- Being part of a family, feeling included in feelings, tasks, and decisions can bring comfort.
- It is easier to teach children about death if we start when they are young to discuss less personal, more distant deaths.

Chapter 11

What You Can Do
for Yourself

Dear Bron,

No, I'm not at all offended, or even surprised, that you can't remember my suggestions about how to help yourself. You sound very normal! Concentrating is often difficult when we're grieving, and so is remembering. After all, do you always remember every word I say?

Writing things down often helps us remember. However, rereading all of these letters may be too much, and smaller amounts of information may be easier to retain. So, I've attached a short summary of what has been in other letters, so you can use it to remind yourself of what might be helpful.

Take care of yourself. You're making progress through this grief, even if it feels rather slow to you.

Talk to you soon,

Love,

_____

SOMETIMES when you're grieving you may feel overwhelmed by everything that seems to be going on. This chapter summarizes various aspects of grief and suggestions for helping yourself. Please use it to review what is happening to you as you grieve, and to remind yourself of what might help you.

Recognize Your Feelings

Grief is a normal response to loss. When you are grieving you may feel sad, angry, lonely, depressed, relieved, numb, empty, hurt, abandoned, guilty, and have many, many other painful feelings. It may help to try to identify the feelings you have.

After a time you may find yourself feeling somewhat reconciled to your loss, even if only grudgingly. Eventually you may feel more at peace and confident that you have survived and even healed—at least somewhat—from your grief. You may even develop a realization that from your grief you have grown in strength, wisdom, and compassion.

Understand Your Reactions

You may:

- need to tell the story over and over
- have disturbed sleeping and eating patterns
- see and hear the one who died
- notice that you and others seem to grieve differently
- have different sexual needs from those of your partner
- be fearful of the future
- find it difficult to concentrate
- feel unable to make decisions
- be anxious about new roles and relationships

These and many other feelings and reactions may occur when you are grieving.

Remember the Stages of Grief

You may find that some of these feelings are stronger at different stages in your grief:

1. *Disbelief* and shock may be stronger during the first month or two after the death.
2. *Pain* and distress may increase during the second month and be particularly strong until six to eight months after the death.
3. *Healing* and reorganization may start to be more noticeable six to eight months after the death.

You will go back and forth between many emotions and all the stages for quite some time. Time alone won't heal your grief; you have to complete your grief work.

Remember the Tasks of Grieving

You need to:

1. Believe the death really happened.
2. Go through the pain of your grief.
3. Learn to live without the one who died.

Many of the feelings and reactions you're experiencing are part of the work of completing these tasks. Be patient with the process and be gentle with yourself. Grieving is hard work.

Take Good Care of Yourself

Grief can affect the immune system, and when you are grieving you are more likely to become sick. You may find you catch colds more easily or have recurrences of chronic conditions such as back pain or depression.

Take good care of your health. Ask yourself what you need to nurture yourself physically, emotionally, intellectually, socially, and spiritually. Here are a few answers from other people, some of which may help you:

- eat regularly and healthily
- get enough sleep or rest
- exercise at least three times a week
- spend time outdoors
- spend time with children
- enjoy the people you love
- play with a pet
- listen to music
- pray
- read
- work
- cry
- laugh
- sing
- write to a friend, maybe the person who died
- keep a journal

Let Others Help You

- determine what *you* think would help
- don't let others tell you what to think or feel
- be cautious when people say, "You should . . ."

- find someone who listens to your story
- if people push you to socialize before you feel ready, ask them to ask you again later
- refuse offers to help you give away his clothes or her books until you're ready
- try not to let others talk to you about the one who died as if she or he were completely awful or completely wonderful; most of us are neither
- ask a friend to accompany you to an occasion you used to attend with the one who died
- let a good friend go with you when attending to tasks related to the death
- think of a few chores or errands to suggest when friends ask what they can do to help you
- spend time with someone who can share memories of the one who died

Seek Grief Counseling If

- you don't have anyone to talk to about your grief
- you seem not to be making any progress with your grief
- your main role in life was caring for the person who died
- the circumstances of the death included violence, suicide, or homicide
- you're considering suicide
- you have a chronic depression (also see your physician)
- you had a very poor relationship with the person who died, especially one which might be characterized as a love/hate relationship
- you have had a series of several losses, including this death, very close together
- you simply think it might help. It will.

To find a grief counselor: See chapter 16, on finding help.

Points to Remember

- Grief is a normal response to loss.
- Grief hurts.
- There are many feelings and reactions associated with grief which may not *seem* normal.
- Everyone grieves differently.
- Grief may take a long time and much work.
- Remember the stages and tasks of grief, but don't worry about which stage you're in or which task you're working on. You may be working on all of them at once.
- Take good care of yourself.
- Let others help you.
- Consider grief counseling or support.

Chapter 12

Helping Someone Who Is Grieving

Dear Bron,

How are you doing? We were so sorry to hear that your friend John died. You two have been good friends for so many years, and I can only imagine how you will miss him. Every time I saw John at your house, I enjoyed talking with him. He was such a warm, engaging person, and always interesting.

The last time I saw him was a few months ago when we were staying with you and he and a few other friends from the "old days" came over for dinner. That night he told me many of the details of his illness. He knew the cancer had advanced and that any further treatments didn't offer any real hope. He seemed very realistic, I thought, and apparently reconciled to the fact that he wouldn't live much longer. I was glad to hear you say his last few weeks were comfortable and peaceful. Thank you for calling us last night to tell us about his funeral. I wish we could have been there.

It sounds as if John's death, attending his funeral, and visiting his family and friends stirred up lots of memories and was hard for you. Understandably so, as your grief about John's death has been added to your grief about Elizabeth. It's so hard when major losses come close together. Not that there is any good time for losses, but I have often thought it might be easier to cope if we had some time in between them to recover. What do you think?

And yes, I certainly understand what you mean when you describe some people at John's funeral seeming uncomfortable and not knowing quite what to say to his family. I think you're being too hard on yourself when you say that you should know what to say because you'd just had a similar loss. With every death we experience, maybe we could learn a little more about what might help others, but that isn't what necessarily happens. Even though everyone experiences losses, many people don't know what to say, no matter how few or how many they have experienced.

I think that we'd all like to be able to say just the right words of comfort and support, but maybe our biggest lesson is that those "right words" may not exist. Usually the only way to help is by being willing to stay with people through their grief.

For a while I think you might find that your grieving for Elizabeth seems worse because John's death has stirred up the memories and sadness. But once again, Bron, this means that you're normal! You're responding the way most of us do when someone we love dies—we remember other losses and other times when we felt the way we do now, and we feel some of that pain again.

Hang in there.

Love,

MANY people feel uncomfortable when they're with someone who is grieving. When you are grieving you may notice that some people seem to avoid you, some seem awkward and unsure of what to say or what to do, and some even say something that probably is meant to comfort you but doesn't.

When we recognize how common is the discomfort people feel with those who are grieving, it is helpful to consider what makes it so difficult. Some discomfort occurs because of the situation, some because people aren't sure what to do, and some because of the expectations some people have of what they should be able to do when someone is grieving.

Death, loss, and grief are sad, painful, even devastating experiences. When we spend time with someone who is grieving, we may also be feeling our own grief because we too loved the one who died. When we are hurting, too, it can be hard to reach out to support another.

If we didn't know the person who died, but know and care about those who are grieving, we may be upset because we know they are hurting.

Most important, even if we didn't know well the one who died or don't really know those who are grieving, we may still be distressed, sometimes to a degree that seems out of proportion.

We are able to understand grief at all only because of our own experience: because we have grieved, we have some understanding of grief. So someone else's grief often reopens the floodgates of our own sadness at losing one we love, and our grief complicates our reactions to the one who is grieving.

Also, to the inevitable distress associated with our being with someone who's grieving, we often add our own unrealistic expectation—that we should help the griever feel better. When we consider the pain a person may feel when someone he or she loves dearly dies, most of us recognize that we cannot take away that pain. But, instinctively, we may try.

Many people can give examples of comments others made or things others did when they were grieving that really hurt or made them angry. These comments were probably well intended, and were an attempt to help or comfort the person grieving. If we explore them to understand why they don't help, we may be better able to understand what *might* help.

What Doesn't Help

"Don't cry!"

One woman said she felt her world had fallen apart when her husband was killed, so "Why, when my whole being felt like screaming in pain, did people tell me not to cry?"

Children may be told, "You're too old to be crying." Some girls are told not to cry, although less often and less strongly than boys, who may also be told, "Be a man. Men don't cry."

"You'll feel better if you cry."

The colleague to whom this remark was made said, "Everything seemed so unreal. I felt frozen, almost as if I were dead myself. People seemed to be talking to me through a wall of some kind, and I couldn't really understand what anyone was saying. The idea that either I might cry or feel better seemed totally irrelevant."

"You must be strong!"

Many of us feel overwhelmed, panicked, and unable to function when we're grieving, and these feelings are hard to handle. Being told to be strong may seem to imply that we're not handling our reactions very well and that we should pull ourselves together.

"You'll have other children."

Many parents who have had a child die, or experienced a

stillbirth or a miscarriage have heard this, and cannot believe that anyone would imagine that this could be a comforting remark. Having other children now or in the future never makes up for the one who died.

"You'll get married again."

For someone whose spouse has just died, this sounds like the person and the relationship can just be replaced. Those who are grieving are often deeply offended by this remark, feeling that it seems to trivialize their loss.

"You must be relieved that she's not suffering anymore."

A friend told me how difficult he found this comment after his mother's death. "Of course I'm glad she's not suffering, but why couldn't her suffering end in a cure rather than death? I don't want her to suffer, I just want her here with me."

"It's God's will."

Being told that the reason for your pain is that God willed it does not bring comfort. Many people may already be upset and angry that God didn't stop this death from happening, and now they'll probably be angry with you too for thinking this would be a comforting remark.

"I know how you feel!"

This may be one of the most disturbing comments, and certainly it's one about which many people complain. "No one knows how I feel! No one else is feeling this pain! There's no way *anyone* can know how I feel."

Because we can never truly understand the relationship they shared, we cannot really understand what that person meant to the one who is grieving, nor can we understand what the loss will mean and what their grief is like.

•

Why do these comments hurt? Why do people remember them so clearly—sometimes years later—as causing them more pain when they were already suffering? Why do these attempts to bring comfort and support so often fail?

We certainly don't mean to hurt the person grieving. We want to help, and we want the person to feel better. That's why these remarks hurt: because of our unrealistic expectation that we *can* make the person feel better.

The comments that people are most hurt by seem to be those that tell people how to feel, how to behave, and how to cope, or explain to them what happened, why it happened, and why they shouldn't feel as bad as they do. The usual problem with comments that try to give us reasons or explanations is that we aren't reasonable or rational when we're in pain.

Our expectation that we need to make the grieving person feel better is usually what makes us uncomfortable and ineffective with grievers. If we think our role is to make the grieving person feel better, we will always be frustrated. We won't succeed, and when we try to make them feel better we may upset and irritate them.

What Can We Do?

Recognizing that we can't make people feel better is where we start; that should help us not to offer some of the comments that can be so hurtful. Then we can try to help by our presence and by trying to understand what the grieving person is experiencing. Rather than seeing our role as being able to "fix it"—that is, to make the person better—we can try to "be there"—that is, to be with him or her and try to understand his or her grief.

Being present, staying with, or being a companion to someone is both simple and difficult. Most of us find it easier to talk to than to listen. Most of us find it easier to give advice than to hear someone cry. To really be present, to listen, to hear, to try to imagine the pain someone is feeling, is a hard task for most people. If you hear someone else's pain, you may feel it, and thus you are leaving yourself open and vulnerable to hurt.

How You Can Help

Initially, either when the person just experienced the loss or when you are first hearing about the grief, you can be most helpful by listening. Listen, with concern and patience and without judging, explaining, or advising, to anything and everything the person says. Try harder to understand than to explain. Try to understand how the grieving person is feeling and what this grief is like for him or her. It's usually a good idea not to talk too much. You might say simply, "I'm sorry."

At other times, perhaps later, you might try the following suggestions.

Ask about their loss. Don't be afraid to ask about what happened, to mention the person who died, or to encourage them to talk about the person who died. Don't be afraid to ask how they are feeling, and be prepared to hear their answers.

Remember. When I was a very young student nurse, I told my head nurse that I didn't know what to say in a letter to the parents of a pediatric patient who had died. Her advice? "Give them a memory. Tell them something you liked, enjoyed, or admired about their daughter or something you experienced or shared with her that you will remember." I still value and use this advice, in letters and in conversations.

"He always loved classical music, and we used to argue all the time about the music I liked. But whenever I hear Mozart, I think of how much I learned from him."

"Do you remember how we laughed when she told us about trying out for the school play? Her imitations of the others were so funny!"

"Whenever I make that chicken and lemon dish I think of

him. He always brought it to the holiday party at the office."

Remember, and mention, days that were special for the person who died, such as birthdays, anniversaries, and holidays. Anna used to make a small Christmas tree for her Grandpa's grave because "it made Grandma happier."

Tony felt nervous and a little awkward about calling the parents of a former colleague on the first anniversary of his death, because "I didn't want to stir up sad memories for them." But when he called, they had just returned from Mass and visiting their son's grave and were delighted that he had remembered. Tony said, "Why did I worry about reminding them? Did I really think they would forget?"

Ask how you can help. You might want to assist with practical matters. Offer to "come over and help," especially with tasks which may be difficult.

"When you're ready to sort through her clothes, would you like me to help?"

"Do you want me to come over and help you go through all the paperwork for the insurance?"

You could also help them identify the roles the person played and encourage them to consider how they'll fill in the gaps.

Don't add extra burdens. Sometimes it helps us to hear about how other people handled situations similar to those we struggle with, and sometimes it doesn't.

Lucy commented that she received a great deal of very practical help from her neighbors after her husband's death. She then said, "But I paid a big price for their help. For example, someone said, 'Let me come and help you with transferring the car from your husband's name. I know how to do that because when my sister died . . .' and then I heard all about her sister's death. Someone else said, 'I know how to complete the insurance forms, because when my husband died . . .' and I had to hear the story of his illness and death and her difficulties since then."

Lucy felt selfish and ungrateful because she didn't want to hear about other people's losses, but she could hardly manage her own grief and couldn't bear to hear all these other stories. It might be better to wait for the one grieving to say, "How do other people manage when this happens?" Or you might say, "Would it help you to know what my brother did in similar circumstances?"

If you have a suggestion because of a similar experience, you might say, "When my cousin's child died in a car wreck, their whole family found support through Compassionate Friends." This will probably be heard better than "You must call Compassionate Friends. When my cousin's child died . . ."

Keep in touch. Grieving is often a very lonely time. In addition to missing the person who died, some people who are grieving find that others stay away from them, probably for many reasons, some of which we have already discussed. And some grieving people are reluctant to contact others or just don't have the energy. Perhaps you can help the grieving person renew old ties and find new contacts. You might suggest activities you can do together. Is there a social event she or he used to attend with the person who died? Perhaps you could offer to go to the potluck supper at the temple with him, or perhaps she'd like you to accompany her when she goes to the next PTA meeting—the first one she's gone to without him. Remember that holidays and anniversaries can be especially difficult; you might offer your support at these special times.

Find out what they *want.* Because we all grieve differently, it's important to understand what the grieving person wants—it may be something you've not thought of, or something which *you*'re sure wouldn't help. Some people may want to visit her grave, or to pray, either alone, with you, or at a service. Some may want to take flowers to where his ashes are strewn, or to listen to the music she liked. Others may want to read over his letters or look at old photos. Ask the person what they would like, what they think seems to help, or what has helped at other times when they have been grieving.

Respect privacy. Some people really want to be left alone completely; others may want company and conversation, but want to grieve alone. For some, grief is too intimate an experience to share with others. How much, if at all, people wish to share depends upon many things, including their relationship with the one who died, their relationship with you, and their individual styles. Some people really need to withdraw into themselves, almost as if the pain that they need to heal is so deep, they cannot bare it to another.

Offer encouragement. People who are grieving often need to be encouraged to take care of themselves. When someone you care about is grieving, try to encourage him or her to eat properly, exercise, spend time outside, and see a doctor if they need to.

Don't just consider physical health, ask about their resources for emotional and social support and spiritual strength.

Pay attention to danger signs, such as weight loss, poor personal hygiene, or inability to function. Perhaps you could explore resources in your community which you might suggest. Try not to give advice, but point out any progress you've seen them make—and keep in touch.

Points to Remember

- The most important way to help someone who is grieving is to listen.
- Pay attention and listen with concern and patience, without judging or advising.

- Ask fewer questions, give less advice, and offer more empathy and more silence.
- Listen for what people say about themselves and help them tell their stories.
- Remember we can never know how another person feels, no matter how close we are to that person or how similar our own experience.

Chapter 13

Grief in the Workplace

Dear Bron,
*How are you doing? I kept thinking about you today.
Next week I'm giving a presentation on grief in the workplace, and when I was reviewing my notes it occurred to
me that we hadn't talked about this aspect of grief very
much. Maybe we hadn't paid much attention to this topic
because you own the company? Maybe as the boss you
have different issues than others? Or maybe you have a
different perspective on the same issues?*

*Anyway, I thought I'd share some ideas with you,
because sooner or later, we all have to deal with grief at
work—either our own or someone else's. Thinking about
how we might respond to this situation before it happens
seems better than waiting until there's a crisis.*

Let me know what you think of this.

Love,

WHAT happens at work when we are grieving? How do we respond when a coworker is grieving? What should we do, say, or

expect from ourselves, our coworkers, and our managers? How does our grief affect our work? What can a manager do when confronted with grief in the workplace?

Usually these questions are not asked in a workplace until someone *is* grieving, and even then, they may not be asked aloud. Instead many people worry about these issues, wonder how others are coping, feel uncomfortable, and hope the issue will go away. Then when it does go away they are left feeling somewhat relieved but also vaguely unsatisfied.

What Happens When You Are Grieving?

Jake's colleagues knew his mother had been seriously ill with cancer for two years. He had made several short visits to be with her during particularly difficult times, such as when she had surgery and during the initial chemotherapy treatments. Recently Jake had been away from work for ten days to be with his mother as she died and to arrange and attend the services. When he returned to work, no one mentioned his being away or his mother's death.

"It was unbelievable! These are people I've worked with for more than three years. I've heard about their families, weddings, new babies, divorces, but no one said even one word to me about my mother."

For many people, returning to work after a death is very difficult. Some fear their sadness will interfere with their ability to concentrate; others just find the whole purpose of their work seems irrelevant. Some don't want colleagues to ask about the death because they fear they may cry, and tears will seem weak or unprofessional. Some, like Jake, are hurt because people seem to ignore their loss.

What Can You Do?

There is no one single way to behave at work when you are grieving. How you handle returning to work or responding to colleagues depends upon many factors, including how you're managing your grief generally and, more specifically, the relationships you have at work.

If you have worked for years with a group of warm, compatible people, you may count your coworkers among your friends. Maybe you've supported some of them through personal as well as professional crises, or even situations similar to your loss and grief now. If you've worked there only a short time, don't know the members of the group very well, and maybe don't like those you do know, you may feel they are the last people in the world who would give you any support, even if you wanted it from them. These are extremes, and more likely you'll think your group is a mixture of people you know, like, and admire, and others you don't. It's also possible that you have no real knowledge of, or relationship with, anyone at work.

You might be able to predict how people you know well will respond, but not necessarily. Sometimes the way people respond to your grief may surprise you. Sometimes the surprise is a pleasant one, sometimes it's not.

No matter how well or how poorly you may know your coworkers, it is most important to determine what you think would be helpful to *you*. If you take off a few days of bereavement leave, consider what it might be like when you return to work. Then consider what you think would be best for you. Do you want to take off more time? Do you want people to recognize your loss? How? With cards, letters, flowers, a brief word of sympathy, a long lunchtime discussion of what happened? You can't control what others will do, of course, but if you think about what might happen, you may be able to influence some behavior.

Ken's father had been sick for a long time before his death. Several days after his father died, Ken called his supervisor, saying he was ready to come back to work but was really tired.

"Over the last few days I've talked with every relative and friend my dad ever had—it feels like there were thousands. Many of them came for the services, and those who didn't get here phoned me several times. I've been talking so much about Dad's illness and death that I'm exhausted. I know folks at work will want to know how things went, but I'm so worn out I don't think I can take it if anyone starts asking me questions. I really need to switch gears a little. But they're good people and I don't want to offend them. Some of them were so helpful to me while he was sick. Some even came by the house and to the funeral."

Later that day, Ken's boss said to the staff, "I spoke with Ken again today. He sounded weary and I guess we can all understand how exhausted he must be since his father's death. He told me he really appreciates all the help and support you've given him. He hopes we'll understand that he doesn't want to talk about it when he returns to work next week. I think it's important to respect his wish, and I hope you all will. At the same time I don't want him to think that I'm ignoring his loss. I plan to write him a note expressing my sympathy and concern, and I wondered if anyone else had any ideas?"

This sounds very neat and tidy, and for Ken it was. However, it often isn't like this. Ken was an extremely self-aware person, he and his supervisor had worked well together for many years, and both had known for a long time that Ken's father was dying. Many of us might not be quite so clear about our needs, have such a good relationship with our supervisor, or have been able to plan, at least in our minds, for quite a while before a death.

You may realize that your colleagues' responses to your grief are not what you would prefer. They may ignore your loss when you want it recognized. They may want to hear every last detail when right now you can't bear to go over the whole scene even one more time. They may want to hug you and cry with you, while you feel that's inappropriate at the office. Or you may be afraid that if they cry, you will too, and you don't wish to spend a whole day at work with reddened eyes and clutching your handkerchief.

You may decide that although the way your coworkers are responding isn't what you'd choose to have them do, you can put up with it. If not, you may want to say something, either directly, although this may be even more distressing for you, or through your supervisor or one of your colleagues.

"I wonder if you could let people know that they don't need to tiptoe around me? They seem to be nervous that I might burst into tears. I'm actually managing quite well, and it feels good to be back at work."

"Do you think you could let people know that I'm feeling a little fragile? I'm fine if they just say they're sorry about his death, and leave it at that. But when they get all emotional and want to hug and cry with me, I fall apart and I really don't want that at work."

It may also be helpful to contact your Employee Assistance Program (EAP) office about bereavement resources, including brochures on grief in the workplace, which might be helpful for you, your coworkers, and your supervisor.

When a Colleague Is Grieving

Diane returned to her office after lunch and heard a colleague on the phone with a client, giving vague and even inaccurate information about one of the services offered through their company. Diane grabbed the phone, tried to soothe the client's anger at the confusing response he'd received, and clarified several questions he had. When she hung up, Diane said, "What on earth's the matter with you? Half of what you told that person wasn't true, and he said the rest was so disjointed, he couldn't figure out what you were saying!"

"If you're so smart, you can take *all* the calls!" her colleague said angrily, and stormed out of the room.

About ten minutes later he returned and said, "This is a really bad day for me. I can't stop thinking about my sister. Do you think you can cover for me if I go home early?"

"But it's nearly six months since your sister died!" Diane said. "Don't you think you should be able to put in a full day's work by now, and without making so many mistakes? How long do you think the company can keep you on if you can't do your job?"

This is not an easy situation for either person. The one grieving may have been troubled by his newly revived grief, by the possible ramifications of his having annoyed a client, and by Diane's criticism.

Diane was annoyed because of the poor response to a client, concerned about how that could affect the company, and suspicious about anyone having a bad day related to a death that had happened six months ago. Was her colleague trying to take advantage of her?

Diane may know that it's not unusual to grieve for six months, a year, or more. She may know that some days will be worse than others. And she also knows that it's reasonable to expect a person to perform the job he's been hired to do. She may feel resentful that she's always covering for her coworker. How long is he going to keep using his sister's death as an excuse for leaving early? Or she may wonder why he suddenly decided to think about it today, when he has never mentioned it before.

Sometimes we can understand why another person's grief seems suddenly sharp again, but often we can't. Sometimes the griever won't know either, or may not want to talk about it with us. Considering how difficult it can be to know what to say at any time, in any place, to anyone who's grieving, certainly we can understand that it may be even more difficult at work. When you both should be working, how appropriate is it to talk about grief?

In this situation Diane needs some support. Her supervisor may be able to help or may seek support for each of them through their human resource department or employee assistance program.

Managers' Roles

Several important aspects of coping with grief in the workplace may best be addressed by looking at the role and responsibilities of a manager. Some important points to consider are privacy, communication, and flexibility.

With a Grieving Employee

Privacy: Ask the grieving person what information he or she would like communicated and to whom. It's usually better to keep it short and simple, perhaps a brief announcement of what happened, and how the employee would like coworkers to respond, if you know.

"I'm sure you'll all be sorry to hear that Jane's younger brother was killed in a traffic accident last night in her home town. She left this morning to be with her parents. Jane was obviously very upset when she called, which I think we can all understand. She said she plans to be back at work next week, but she's still in shock and isn't sure what she'll be like then or how she'll be able to function."

Try to understand coworkers' reactions, but don't become involved in gossip or speculation, such as wondering if the brother had been drinking.

Communication: It's always important to maintain contact with an employee, especially in a time of crisis, while at the same time respecting an employee's need for privacy. Be sure to recognize the employee's grief and sorrow, and ask if there is any way you can help.

Ask the employee to keep in touch, to let you know how she is doing, and to let you know when she'll be back at work. When she returns to work, reiterate that you'd like to know how she's doing and that she should let you know if she needs any help.

Flexibility: Good managers know the importance of being flexible—it may be their most important quality. When someone is grieving it's often hard to predict how well the person will be able to work, so you may need that flexibility.

You should be prepared for difficulties and have some backup plans if the person can't function as usual. You may need to make "reasonable accommodation" as you would for anyone who is sick: perhaps shorter hours or altered job responsibilities for a while.

Although it is wise for you to be prepared, don't make changes unless you need to. You may find the person functions as usual and doesn't need any extra support. Some people when they're grieving will be able to function well in their usual job, but not be able to adapt to another role, even if that one may seem less stressful to you. Be sure you involve the one who's grieving in the decision-making process.

With Coworkers

How can a manager assist coworkers of the one who is grieving? You might start by considering the same points of privacy, communication, and flexibility, but from a slightly different perspective.

Privacy and information: What do coworkers need to know, and how much should you say? Share only what the person involved has said you may, and keep it short.

Communication and an opportunity to be involved: Depending on the group and the relationships they have with each other and the one who's grieving, it can help to involve staff. You might say: "Perhaps someone would like to do something, maybe buy a plant and a card we can all sign, or make a contribution to a favorite charity? What do you think she would like us to do?"

Depending upon the suggestions that come from the group, you may want to delegate the task to those who worked most closely with her.

Flexibility and altered workload: Because you cannot know how the affected employee may cope, it's appropriate to warn others that you may shift some extra responsibilities to them for a while.

Reactions to death and grief: It is helpful to warn employees that a grieving colleague may stir up their own memories of losses. Try to understand coworkers' reactions, although you may never know how this news has affected them. Remember that your colleague's news may stir up some painful memories for you also.

Recognize your importance as a role model. How you respond to a coworker's loss and grief will be noted and remembered.

When an Employee Dies

When an employee dies, there are many factors that can affect the impact in the workplace. As a manager it is helpful for you to consider how the death will affect the employee's coworkers, the workload, and yourself.

Anticipate the possible effect. The death may reduce coworkers' productivity and motivation. Do you have any flexibility in the workload? Could you delay a project or ask for more help?

Give coworkers a chance to grieve. There are many ways to do this, and how much you become involved—if at all—will vary. Staff might take up a collection and give it to the employee's family or donate it to a charity in honor of the employee. They may decide to go together to the funeral, or a few might go to represent the group. They may offer to pack up any personal items from his desk and take them to the family. They may want to write a group letter to the family expressing their sadness at her death.

Sometimes the circumstances of the death demand more attention, or even crisis intervention.

When Brian, a man in his early forties, had a heart attack at work, everyone in his office was affected. Coworkers saw him collapse, the supervisor called 911, and two colleagues initiated mouth-to-mouth breathing. Brian's colleagues saw the paramedics arrive, insert a tube down his throat to help him breathe, and start an intravenous line to give medications. They watched them carry their colleague out of the office to transport him to the hospital.

The manager called EAP and asked for assistance. By the time the paramedics left, an EAP counselor had already arrived to facilitate an immediate session with everyone in the office. They were still in the session when the supervisor received a message that their colleague was dead.

Many people would be extremely distressed by witnessing a sudden death and a resuscitation attempt such as this one. Having a counselor meet with the whole group, as soon as was possible, helped people start dealing with their shock and distress immediately. This can help the colleagues, as a group and as individuals, to begin to work through what happened, support each other, and avoid more problems later.

Pay attention to the replacement. When you hire a replacement for an employee who died, it is important to notice the reactions of the coworkers to that new employee. If staff seem to be ignoring or even hostile toward the new person, they may still have some feelings related to the death. If problems arise it may be worth considering a possible connection to grief.

When an Employee Is Terminally Ill

If an employee is terminally ill you might want to consider grief support *before* the death, either for the one who is ill, for his or her colleagues, for you as manager, or for all of you. This might sound strange and, depending upon the individual and the group, may be neither necessary nor desirable. There are times, however, when facilitating anticipatory grief in this way can be very helpful to the individual and the group.

Again, the manager has the task of balancing assistance for the one who's ill, support for coworkers, and the need to keep the workplace functioning. Following are some possible strategies for managers when an employee is terminally ill.

Be open about ability to work. Involve a sick employee in discussions about performance and illness. An early and open discussion with the employee about possible options to consider can prevent some of the tensions that might arise. Often the tendency is to wait and have this discussion once a problem arises, but recognizing early that eventually the illness will make it harder for the employee to perform at work may make it easier to plan.

Hold regular discussions with the employee. Discuss how she or he feels, how well she or he is functioning and your observations, including any problems you see, and ask what the person would like to do. After exploring reasonable options, perhaps shorter hours, reduced responsibilities, or a leave of absence, decide on one choice with which you both are reasonably comfortable. Whichever option is chosen should be evaluated regularly to see if it is effective.

Respect privacy. An employee may not want you to disclose anything about his condition, and this should be respected. However, it's reasonable for you as a manager to point out that the employee may need to reconsider such confidentiality under certain circumstances. For instance, if you need to make special arrangements to accommodate his failing health, you will need to justify these arrangements to your supervisor. Also, if co-workers are asked to take on extra responsibilities while the employee who's sick is doing less and less, the coworkers may become resentful if they don't understand the reason.

A manager is not a counselor. Although it is helpful if a manager is concerned and supportive when a worker is seriously ill, the manager (or a coworker) shouldn't try to be the employee's counselor. It's better for both you and the employee if you can offer other resources, perhaps a referral to your Employee Assistance Program or human resources department. There may be support groups or services available both through your organization and in the community, and EAP can assist the employee to explore what might help.

As a manager you may find it very difficult, for a variety of reasons, to work with an employee who is seriously ill. Remember that EAP programs are for managers also. Perhaps you need some supportive guidance for yourself from EAP. It is appropriate to seek advice about how to cope with issues relating to a seriously ill employee. If the employee has asked for privacy, you can still approach EAP and ask for advice for yourself, without identifying the person who is sick.

•

Peter took over as project director of a small agency that was in a shambles. He recruited virtually an entire new staff. They worked closely and intensively to completely redesign their program, and their first project was an immediate success. The team worked hard over the next few years, further strengthening the program and gaining increased respect and visibility. Their success and the accolades they received, as well as the pure fun and hard work, were exhilarating and exhausting.

But from the beginning the group was beset by interpersonal and disciplinary problems. Peter had recruited the best people he could find, and each excelled professionally, but the group had never worked together before. Tensions developed among the workers.

Peter hired a management consultant, who conducted a workshop to help the group clarify each person's expectations, roles, and responsibilities. There was noticeable improvement within the group, especially an increased appreciation of what each had to contribute and a greater respect for each other's styles. Peter described what happened next.

"In about the fourth year of the project, Maria (one of the professional staff) was diagnosed with terminal cancer. At first, we took a business-as-usual approach to her illness. But over time this was less and less effective. I was concerned about two issues. First, since I had not worked with a terminally ill colleague before, I was unsure what was appropriate behavior, and what I should say to her about her illness. Was it okay to ask how she was feeling? Might this invite in-depth comments about what was happening to her that I really didn't want to hear? How should I treat performance issues? Should she and I have a discussion up front, or should I handle problems as they arose?

"Second, her terminal illness complicated a somewhat delicate truce in the office. I had spent considerable time trying to sort through various roles, responsibilities, professional relationships, and performance issues. I did not know how to handle all this, and again asked our management consultant for advice."

The consultant referred Peter to another consultant who, after meeting with Peter and Maria, facilitated a grief workshop for the staff. Peter described the process, which helped all members of the group focus on issues of loss and grief in their own lives, on what each thought would be his or her fears when diagnosed with a terminal illness, and how she or he would want to be treated by colleagues.

Peter commented: "The sharing of the pain of loss which occurred in those sessions made it possible—in a magical kind of way, I don't know how else to describe it—for the group to talk about Maria's illness with Maria actively engaged in the discussion. It would have been impossible to do this without her willing and active participation. She wanted this discussion, had the same—or similar—concerns that we did, and the workshop broke the dam of pent-up anxieties we were all holding. We said and did things that we could not have otherwise.

"First we had an open discussion about what Maria wanted from us, which was clear and simple. She liked her work, wanted to stay involved, and feared that we would shut her out and begin to ignore her. We agreed to keep her involved as long as her health permitted. She also said she welcomed questions about how she was feeling, as long as they weren't too persistent or intrusive, and appreciated opportunities to talk about how things were going for her. This openness became easier for all of us, and Maria and I became closer.

"Next we had an open conversation about how we as a group would handle Maria's obligations. We agreed that as much and for as long as she wanted she would continue to do the things she had always done. We agreed that there were going to be times when she would not be able to manage and the group would pick up the slack.

"The combined results of the roles and responsibilities workshop and the grief workshop were that interpersonal relationships in the office improved, morale soared, and the project continued to flourish. The two workshops provided unique opportunities for each member of our group to connect and bond with other members.

"Having said this, I don't want to get too syrupy. Offices are not families. Each person in a workplace has distinct and clear roles and responsibilities. For an office to be successful, each one has to do his or her share. Both the roles and responsibilities workshop and the grief workshop provided opportunities to address real problems affecting office performance. These sessions improved individual and group performance, and strengthened our project."

Peter's description of the two workshops and their effect illustrate the role a manager can play in providing grief education and support in a workplace. The role of any manager is to manage a group of people who work together. An issue that affects the performance of one worker or leads to tension and anxiety that affect one or several members of the group is of concern to a manager.

Addressing grief in the workplace may seem to be humane or compassionate, or unnecessary or even intrusive, and sometimes any or all of those adjectives might apply. However, in some circumstances, addressing grief may result in improved working relationships and increased efficiency.

Points to Remember

- When *you*'re grieving, people at work may not respond in ways you wish they would.

- Consider asking your supervisor or a close colleague to let others know what you need.
- When a *colleague* is grieving, don't ignore the loss or his or her grief.
- Consider ways to offer your sympathy and concern that might be most acceptable to your colleague. Generally, a few words or a short note are appropriate in the workplace.

For Managers

- As a manager, you need to balance your support of a grieving or seriously ill employee with your responsibility to keep the workplace functioning.
- Be prepared to offer resources for support and guidance to the grieving employee, coworkers, and yourself, through your EAP program and resources available in the community.
- For a grieving employee, consider his/her privacy, communicate regularly, try to be flexible with work, and involve him/her in decisions.
- When someone is grieving, watch for danger signs, such as weight loss, poor personal hygiene, or an inability to function. It may be necessary to insist on an EAP referral.

144

- Anticipate the effect of one person's grief, illness, or death on others in the group, and consider opportunities for coworkers to receive support.
- Consider EAP advice and support for yourself.

Chapter 14

Grief and AIDS

Dear Bron,

I had a call from my friend Ryan last night. Do you remember him? He and I worked together for several years, and he came here for lunch when you were visiting us. Then he moved back to California and I went to see him after my last visit to see you.

Ryan's been HIV positive as long as I've known him, and it was when he developed AIDS that he returned home to California. He called because another friend had just died of AIDS.

We talked about what it's been like for him having so many friends die during the last several years. For Ryan, and for many other gay men, it's not unusual to go to several funerals a month. His partner, friends, extended family, and indeed whole community are affected by HIV.

For Ryan—and for me—one of the hardest parts of his becoming sicker is that he doesn't always remember clearly. This time we agreed that I'd also write to him about what he and I talked about. I'm sending you a copy of what I sent him, in case you too have a friend dealing

with AIDS who needs this information. If you don't now,
you probably will eventually.
Every time we talk, I notice how well you sound!

Love,

WHAT is it like when someone you love dies of AIDS? Is the grief the same as when a death is from other causes? What support do you receive?

What happens when you belong to a community where HIV infection rates are high? In the United States the impact of the AIDS pandemic was first seen in gay communities in big cities; there it is not uncommon to know dozens of people who have died of AIDS. In some countries in Africa a grandmother may take care of twenty-five grandchildren because all of her children and their spouses have died of AIDS.

If you are also infected with HIV, how does your grief from one person dying of AIDS or the accumulated grief from many deaths affect you? How can you take care of yourself?

Grief is always affected by many and differing factors. If two families are killed in a car accident, or five hundred people drown when a ferryboat sinks, or ten women in one hospital die during childbirth, or one person dies saving six children from a fire, factors affecting the grief associated with each situation would vary. In grief associated with AIDS deaths, the diagnosis, issues of contagion, social attitudes, and number of other people dying of AIDS may affect the grief process.

Grief can affect the immune system, making anyone who is grieving more susceptible to illness. Since the immune systems of those infected with the Human Immunodeficiency Virus (HIV) are already being attacked by the virus, the accumulated impact of HIV *and* grief can make people with HIV particularly vulnerable to other illnesses.

148

Grief and AIDS

It is important for those affected by HIV—either because of their own infection or that of others they love—to consider how best to manage the associated grief.

•

There are many and sometimes seemingly endless losses for those affected by the HIV/AIDS pandemic. The most obvious and most painful loss is when someone you love and with whom you share an important relationship dies of AIDS. This might be your spouse, partner, parent, child, sibling, or close friend. This is a major loss, and you need to grieve the way we all need to grieve any major loss in life.

In addition, you may also be affected by deaths of those whom you knew less well or even not at all. Maybe someone with whom you had chatted in the doctor's waiting room dies. Or you hear of the death of a person you sat next to at a memorial service for a mutual friend. Some people who are infected can tell you how many people have died of AIDS in their own community, in the country, and in the world. They do not know those people, but those deaths have a greater impact on them than on those who are not infected.

This is not surprising. Anyone diagnosed with *any* illness will become aware of many others with similar diagnoses. They may have been ill for a long time, but we didn't know this, or didn't pay much attention to their illness. Now we seem to meet many people with diagnoses similar to ours. We may seek them out—maybe to ask how they are coping—or perhaps we meet them at places where we go because of our diagnosis, such as a clinic.

Some aspects of grief associated with a death from AIDS are the same as with any other death. But here we will consider some possible differences relating to specific circumstances.

Many People Who Die of AIDS Are Young

Most people infected with HIV and dying of AIDS are in their twenties, thirties, or forties. In an earlier chapter we discussed the fact that deaths of young people are often harder to cope with than those of older people.

Ellen was in her early forties when her son died of AIDS. "If I'd thought much about death I would have said I expected to die before Joel, but he died first. This doesn't make sense. Why should I have lots more time, when he hardly had a chance to start living yet?"

Also, the years between twenty and forty are when many people have children and are most productive in their work and within their family and communities. For a survivor of someone who dies in those years, there may be issues related to income and parenting to be considered.

Jane was not infected with HIV, but when her former husband died of AIDS she was concerned about how she could manage without even the meager amount of child support he had been sending. "But what's worse is that I don't know what to say to the children about why Ed died. I don't want to tell them about HIV, but I don't want to lie to them either. And I'm afraid they may hear it from someone else. You know how people talk."

Distressing Symptoms and Difficult Treatments

There has been a great deal of knowledge gained about HIV and the opportunistic diseases such as pneumonia or tuberculosis that may accompany HIV infection. There are now some medicines that reduce the ability of the virus to reproduce, treatments to control or cure some opportunistic infections, and ways to provide more comfort by relieving distressing symptoms such as pain, diarrhea, and coughing.

Some people do not have access to treatment or good care, some symptoms can be very difficult to control, and sometimes the treatments themselves can be uncomfortable and distressing. The grief of the survivors may be affected by memories of how the person who died struggled, even suffered.

Fred said of his partner who had died a year and a half before, "I knew he wanted to keep trying anything which might help. But when I think about what he went through with some treatments, I wish he hadn't tried them. It was easier to see him die than to see him go through what he did."

Discomfort, Fear, Stigma, and Isolation

In many societies conversations about sex or death are neither common nor comfortable. Discussions about HIV often include sex *and* death, which makes the conversation even more uncomfortable. In some countries discussions about HIV may also cover homosexual activity or illegal drug use, which further adds to many people's discomfort. It is not too surprising that people may avoid conversations or situations that include HIV/AIDS.

Some people know very little about HIV/AIDS and are disturbed by anything that is new. Others have gathered their knowledge of HIV/AIDS from the "supermarket medical journals" where information is less factual than sensational. In that case they may have many unfounded fears and inaccurate beliefs about how they might "catch AIDS" from the survivor.

HIV-related illness can be devastating, but the stigma attached to this illness can be worse. There is often tremendous anxiety when people tell their families, employers, and friends about being HIV positive. There are incidents of people with HIV losing their jobs, health insurance, and the support of their friends, families, and faith communities. The discomfort and fear some people experience and the stigma they perceive can lead them to stay away from people with HIV/AIDS. The resulting abandonment and isolation of many people with HIV/AIDS also may be experienced by those who survive them. And people who have HIV or are grieving a death from AIDS may be reluctant to mention the diagnosis because they don't know how others will react, so they isolate themselves.

Barbara and Alan grew up in a small town and lived next door to each other. They were close friends in kindergarten and elementary school, fierce enemies in junior high, and then friends again in high school. After graduation they went in different directions, Barbara to Washington, D.C., and Alan to San Francisco, where each visited the other a few times. During those visits, and whenever they went home for holidays, they picked up their friendship again very easily.

Alan told Barbara that he was gay before he told his family. He told her when he was diagnosed as HIV positive and asked for her support when he told his mother he had AIDS. And Barbara helped Alan's mother take care of him in California when he was dying.

Returning home after his death, Alan's mother told her friends that Alan had died of leukemia. She was overwhelmed with grief, but felt unable to ask her minister or her friends for support. She was afraid that if she started to talk to them about Alan, she might let slip that he had AIDS. She thought they would be horrified.

She still doesn't know how people in her community would have reacted, because she never told them. Instead, she did her grief work by writing in a journal every day and in phone calls with Barbara every week.

When we consider the tasks of grieving we can appreciate

how difficult it can be to complete those tasks without talking about our loss. Isolation can lead to prolonged and difficult grief.

Isolation may also happen when the significance of a person's relationship with the one who died is not acknowledged. For a gay couple, when one dies, the other may experience disenfranchised grief. If their relationship was not known, not accepted, or not perceived as significant, the survivor may feel that his grief is not allowed.

For some survivors, their grief is complicated because they are so distressed by the behaviors that led to the person becoming infected with HIV. When Martha was dying of AIDS, her sister refered to her as "the bad apple." Dismay, disappointment, and anger at Martha's drug use added to her sister's pain and grief.

Survivors may also feel grief or guilt if they are responsible for infecting the person who died. This may be particularly difficult when a baby is born infected because the mother (or both parents) is infected, and the child dies before either parent.

Taking Care of Your Own Grief

The following suggestions for grieving a death—or deaths—from AIDS are for anyone who knows many people who either are infected now or have already died of AIDS. These suggestions are especially important for anyone who is HIV infected as well.

Recognize Your Limits

Recognize the limits of what you can do. Learn to say "I can't" to additional responsibilities when your physical energy is low and "I need help" in situations you cannot emotionally handle alone. Recognize signs of excessive stress and the limits of your endurance, and say "I need time to myself."

Wilson, who was not infected with HIV, worked as a volunteer with an AIDS service organization, driving clients to doctors' appointments and to church services.

"I don't know most of the clients well, but sometimes I feel really upset when the coordinator calls from the office to say someone doesn't need transportation anymore because he died."

Wilson gradually realized he would function longer and better in his volunteer role if he took regular breaks from it.

People who are infected usually find support from others who are HIV positive, but they may need to consider reducing this contact at times to care better for themselves.

Jean joined a group for women who were HIV positive. After attending for three weeks (she had only known she was positive for six weeks) she dropped out because "I was afraid to ask what happened to so-and-so this week. I didn't want to hear that she was sicker or had died. I've heard more than enough about people dying, and I certainly don't want to get to know people who aren't going to be around next week."

In Jean's case, the timing was wrong for her. Several months later she tried the group again and this time she stayed.

Ryan belonged to a group of HIV-positive volunteers in a research program at a major medical center. Each month members of the group would attend the clinic for interviews and testing by the research team and for a support group. He said, "Then some members died, and we had others join our group. Over the next few years we had other deaths and other new members, but I always watched the original members more closely. When the only other survivor of our original group died, I left. I couldn't take any more."

Ryan realized the burden of being "the last one left." The pain of so many deaths now outweighed any benefits he might gain from the group. It was time for him to move on.

Grief and AIDS

Take Care of Yourself

Take care of yourself physically, through excercise, sleep, and good nutrition; spiritually, by finding opportunities to nurture your spiritual strength; and emotionally and socially, with people you love and through a support group.

Find a Support Group

Most people who are grieving a death from AIDS of someone they love find it easier to ask for support from those who have experienced similar grief. An AIDS service organization can help you find a grief group or support group to join either before the death, or afterward. Ask them what grief groups or bereavement services they—or others in the community—offer.

If you are infected yourself, you might need two groups—a grief group for support as you grieve for someone else's death and another group to help you cope with your own diagnosis. Or perhaps you can find a group that can offer you support with both those needs.

Work with Others

When people die of AIDS, it is not hard to imagine those who survive them being overwhelmed by grief and sadness. It is much harder to imagine how anyone can find hope or healing of their grief. In difficult circumstances people may find hope through purpose, spirituality, and a sense of connectedness.

Purpose: Many AIDS organizations were started by people grieving a death from AIDS. They joined with others, usually to develop educational programs about avoiding infection or to provide services and support for people with AIDS and their

155

families. Many who work in these organizations find purpose, hope, and meaning in what they do.

Paul was twenty-seven, looked about sixteen, and was infected with HIV. He was a very effective speaker in an AIDS-education program for teenagers, and he found great satisfaction and renewed strength through his work.

"If telling my experiences helps some of these kids think *before* they take a chance of becoming infected, then I'm really making a difference. This is probably the most important thing I've done in my whole life. When I die, I want you to be sure that my obituary mentions my work with this group."

Several other HIV-infected speakers agreed that working in this program gave them a sense of purpose. They felt valued for their contribution, moved by the way many of the young people responded to them, and found they had more energy and enthusiasm for living.

Spirituality: Facing the many deaths, other losses, and much grief associated with HIV/AIDS raises spiritual questions for many people. Why does this virus kill so many young people, leaving their children with little or no support? Sexual activity can create new life, but with the addition of HIV/AIDS it can also spread death. Why did this happen? I was always faithful, but my husband wasn't. He got infected but is still well. Why are my baby and I dying because of what he did? Why do people suffer?

For those who are religious, their questions will reflect their beliefs. Why does God allow an illness like this to exist? Why did God let all of my children die of AIDS? How can I take care of ten grandchildren alone? Has God abandoned me?

Answers to these questions are not easy to find, and one person's answers may not help another. It is easier to imagine the pain or fear or loneliness behind these questions. When we work with others to try to relieve this pain, fear, and loneliness, we can develop a supportive environment. This can be a safe place to voice these questions, maybe find some answers, and feel comforted that others are struggling with similar issues.

Facing these issues leads many to consider their spiritual resources, and to share them with each other. When asked, "Where do you find your spiritual strength?" many will answer, "From the people I help care for, and from their family members."

Connectedness: Relationships and a sense of belonging are essential in our lives. Individuals who work together confronting life-and-death issues in a time of crisis often find support in feeling connected to others struggling with similar issues.

The effects of the AIDS pandemic have been, are, and will continue to be, devastating. Sometimes it is hard to imagine that anything good can come out of it. But many persons who work in this field have been privileged to develop strong supportive relationships with others whom they might never have met otherwise. Good relationships nurture our spirits and can be a source of comfort, support, healing, and hope.

Points to Remember

- Grief can affect the immune system, so anyone who is grieving is more susceptible to illness. Grieving can make those infected with HIV particularly vulnerable.
- It is important to find appropriate grief support.
- The discomfort around HIV/AIDS may lead to the isolation of those grieving a death from AIDS.

- Trying to hide that AIDS was the cause of death can complicate the survivors' grief work.
- Usually we find great support in being with others who are facing similar issues. But sometimes it may help to limit this contact if the burdens outweigh the benefits.
- Hope may be found in goals, spirituality, and connectedness.

Chapter 15

Finding Help

With Expected Grief

MOST of this book has been about what is sometimes referred to as "normal grief." I always think that the word "normal," when applied to grief, needs some definition and clarification. We may find that very little about grief feels normal. Indeed, many of our reactions and behaviors when we grieve seem strange and abnormal. If you, like many others who grieve, are troubled by the use of "normal" try using the word "expected" instead.

Losses are an expected part of everyone's life. Grief is an expected response to loss. Grieving people may be expected to experience some or all of the feelings, reactions, concerns, and questions that have been described in this book.

Grief is not an aberration, a sign of being poorly adjusted, or a mental illness or psychiatric disorder. So why do people need help with grief? Because grief hurts. But in many cases the help that we need is nearby.

Many people receive good support from families and friends when grieving. Many receive support within their faith community. They find counsel from a concerned rabbi, minister, priest, or spiritual teacher, guidance and comfort in the teachings and practices of their faith, and fellowship within the community. Many churches and temples offer groups, materials, family and youth programs, pastoral care teams, and other resources for those dealing with loss and grief.

The support that many receive from families and friends or from other groups to which they belong may be a common part of life in their community—so much so that the grieving person may not even be aware of how much help he or she receives.

But sometimes the support isn't there, and sometimes the community does not help us. Grief is often not well understood in Western society, nor is it well tolerated. When you're grieving you may feel strong pressure to get over your loss quickly and not to talk about your sadness. In that case you might need to seek help and guidance through a grief counseling service.

Having been involved in hospice work for so many years, I know how helpful bereavement care can be. Many hospice programs offer a wide range of services to the communities they serve, including bereavement support services. They may offer information about the grieving process and support for people as they grieve and adjust to loss. Many offer grief groups, regular supportive contact with trained bereavement volunteers, and resources and referrals for people with extra needs.

Some hospices will provide these services for anyone in their community who needs it; other hospices provide bereavement services only for family and friends of people who died in their hospice program, but will refer you to an appropriate resource.

To find hospice programs in your community, look under "Hospices" in the Yellow Pages of your phone book. Or call the office of the National Hospice Organization (NHO) at 1-800-658-8898. NHO maintains a listing of hospice programs across the country and can tell you which are close to you.

To identify further resources for grief support, look in your phone book under local and state government services. Grief programs or bereavement support services are not usually listed, so call departments such as Mental Health Services, Family Services, or Aging Services. You could also try local numbers for the AARP Widowed Persons Service, the American Cancer Society, Candlelighters, or Compassionate Friends.

You can also contact local mental health services, employee assistance programs, pastoral counseling centers, churches, temples, mosques, and other community groups to see if they offer bereavement care.

It can be helpful to seek out specialized support—perhaps a grief group, made up of those with similar losses, such as those for widows and widowers, or for parents of young children. Or perhaps by the specific cause of death: AIDS, Alzheimer's, or Sudden Infant Death Syndrome (SIDS). For children, age-specific groups can be helpful.

However, it can also be very helpful to mix these groups together. No matter what the cause of death, our relationship to the person who died, and our situation since the death, we all have much in common. It seems to me that grief may be a common denominator between all people. No matter who we are or where we come from, we all experience loss. No matter how we describe, deny, or express grief, we all feel sadness and pain. Because of our own experiences we can begin to understand— at least somewhat—another's grief.

Be sure that any counseling service you consider is focused on grief and bereavement, and that any counselor—whether a psychiatrist, psychologist, social worker, mental health worker, minister, or volunteer—has had training and experience in grief and bereavement support.

You are not seeking psychotherapy, you need support and information as you grieve—a normal, expected response to loss.

With Especially Difficult Grief

This book has also referred to situations that might be considered unusual, unexpected, or especially difficult.

We expect that everyone will experience loss and grief during life. We *don't* expect that four of our five children will die of cancer, that our whole family will drown when a boat capsizes, that someone we love who seems to have everything going for him will kill himself, or that most of our community will die of AIDS.

Many of these unexpected and awful, devastating losses will cause especially difficult grief. Other examples of unexpected losses and especially difficult grief include homicide or any death that was violent, even if from natural causes.

You might also be in a situation where your behavior caused the death, intentionally or not. You might have killed someone—perhaps your driving caused a fatal traffic accident, or you took your eyes off a child who then wandered into a street or fell into a pool.

You might also experience many losses at the same time or a series of losses that seem to come one right after the other.

For any especially difficult grief you may need longer, more intensive counseling and help, and the particular circumstances of the grief may best be addressed by specialized resources.

Remember that there are often resources available in your community that you may not know of. If you ask one person or make one call you may discover that others are facing or have faced losses similar to yours.

Start with your own family doctor or clergyperson, a mental health program or pastoral counseling service listed in the phone book, or anyone you know who works in health care or community service programs. They can help you find the resources you need.

Recommended Reading

There are many books on grief, and a visit to your library or a bookstore may surprise you. However, you may find some are too long, and others may not appeal to your interests or tastes.

Here are a few suggestions. These books are fairly short and easily read and therefore suitable for times when you are grieving and/or trying to help another who is grieving. Many of these are old favorites that I turn to again and again—either to reread myself or to give to others.

Grollman, Earl A. *Talking About Death.* Boston: Beacon Press, 1970.

Kushner, Harold. *When Bad Things Happen to Good People.* New York: Avon, 1983.

LeShan, Eda. *Learning to Say Good-Bye: When a Parent Dies.* New York: Macmillan, 1976.[*]

Lewis, C. S. *A Grief Observed.* San Francisco: Harper & Row, 1961, 1989.

Nieburg, H., and A. Fischer. *Pet Loss.* New York: Harper & Row, 1982.

Stein, Sara Bonnett. *About Dying.* New York: Walker, 1974.[*]

• Abbey Press, in St. Meinrad, Indiana, publishes a series called CareNotes. These brief, concise, and attractive booklets are simple but not simplistic, and emphasize "using all one's resources—emotional, physical, mental, spiritual, social—to cope with life's biggest challenges." Grief-related titles include *Getting Through Annual Reminders of Your Loss, Helping a*

---

[*]These are written for children and are excellent. They contain valuable information, are written in easily assimilated language, and are very helpful for children and adults.

Child Grieve, Planning the Funeral of Someone You Love, Taking the Time You Need to Grieve Your Loss, Bearing the Special Grief of Suicide, and *Grieving the Loss of Your Parent.*

• Tom Golden, a counselor in Washington, D.C., has written three booklets: *A Man's Grief: What Is Grief?, Different Paths Toward Healing,* and *Gender and Cultural Differences in Grief.* They are nicely written, easy to read, and very useful. Contact:

Tom Golden, L.C.S.W.
10400 Connecticut Avenue, Suite 514
Kensington, MD 20895

• A series of brochures, *Grief in the Workplace,* developed through the Hospice Council of Metropolitan Washington, D.C., are available through NHO.

• There are many books written for professional grief counselors and/or therapists. Anyone wanting to explore this topic further might want to check the local library. Because of the amount and level of information these books are more easily read when we are not in acute grief. The following few books are written by experts in the field:

Tatelbaum, Judith. *The Courage to Grieve* (New York: HarperCollins, 1984). Many grief books tell a story of personal loss. The author of this book is an experienced, well-respected grief counselor and combines her own story with information and insights gained from her professional role.

Viorst, Judith. *Necessary Losses* (New York: Ballantine, 1986). This book contains much information, research, and details, and is a wonderful resource. This much material on grief may be overwhelming for some, but the author's style makes it easier than one might expect.

Worden, J.W. *Grief Counseling and Grief Therapy* (New York: Springer Publishing Company, 1982). If you really want a textbook—this is the classic.

• For health care professionals who experience many deaths

and losses, the following books are excellent resources for exploring issues related to ongoing loss and grief.

Frankl, V. *Man's Search for Meaning.* New York: Washington Square Press, 1959.

Harper, B. C. *Death: The Coping Mechanism of the Health Professional.* Greenville, South Carolina: Southeastern University Press, 1994.

Parkes, C. M., and R. S. Weiss. *Recovery from Bereavement.* New York: Basic Books, 1983.

Rando, T. *Treatment of Complicated Mourning.* Champaign, Illinois: Research Press, 1993.

• Read the holy books of different religions. People sometimes turn to old, favorite passages and find comfort. New or less familiar materials can also soothe you. Don't necessarily limit yourself to the scriptures of a religion you believe in or are at least familiar with. If you grew up in the Judeo-Christian tradition, you may be surprised by the solace to be found in the Koran or the teachings of Buddha. No matter your religious beliefs—or even if you don't have any—you may find beauty, wisdom, and peace in religious or spiritual writings.

Finding Help and Consolation

One of the best ways to find help may be to look within yourself. When those who are important to us die, we miss them. If we take time to explore just *how* they were important, what we gained from having known them, or what we learned from them, we may be able to see the gifts they gave us.

There may be tangible gifts, such as your grandfather's prayer book or your grandmother's bracelet, but what other gifts can we find? Did your mother share her love of music with you, and has that gift been a source of joy in your life? Did your father encourage you to explore new ideas and opportunities, which brought enriching experiences into your life? Did someone show you how people with very little material wealth can be generous and sharing with others? Did someone dealing with tremendous problems in the community impress you with how one person's courage gives strength to others? Or did someone completely helpless because of debilitating illness show you that accepting help can be done with grace?

Identifying what we received or learned from those who have died can help us find comfort and consolation. We can balance the sadness of our loss with an appreciation of the gifts they gave us. All those gifts will be part of us throughout our lives, and so will those who gave them to us.

I wish you peace and healing from your grief.

WE REMEMBER THEM

At the rising of the sun and at its going down,
we remember them.
At the blowing of the wind and in the chill of winter,
we remember them.
At the opening of the buds and in the rebirth of spring,
we remember them.
At the shining of the sun and in the warmth of summer,
we remember them.
At the rustling of the leaves and in the beauty of autumn,
we remember them.
At the beginning of the year and at its end,
we remember them.
As long as we live, they too will live;
for they are now a part of us,
as we remember them.

When we are weary and in need of strength,
we remember them.
When we are lost and sick at heart,
we remember them.
When we have joy we crave to share,
we remember them.
When we have decisions that are difficult to make,
we remember them.
When we have achievements that are based on theirs,
we remember them.
As long as we live, they too will live;
for they are now a part of us,
as we remember them.

Sylvan Kamens and Jack Riemer in
New Mahzor for the High Holy Days

Points to Remember

- Grief is an expected response to loss, and loss is a part of life.
- With time and work you will find some healing of your grief.
- Take care of yourself, and try to be patient with the grief process.
- Many of us need the support of others when we grieve.
- Help is available.
- Look for and remember the gifts.

Postscript

Dear Reader,

As I complete the final review of this material, I'm very much aware of my current grief concerning recent and ongoing losses, and of the continued value of grief education.

Recently my healthy, active husband, whose energy and productivity suggest someone a decade younger than his actual age, was diagnosed with prostate cancer. Fortunately, all follow-up studies and multiple opinions indicate that the cancer has been found early, that it has not spread beyond the gland, and that with appropriate treatment he has a good chance of complete cure. Nevertheless, there are losses and grief—for him, me, family members, friends, and colleagues.

At the same time we have been struggling with losses affecting my parents-in-law. Although reasonably healthy and active for their eighty-nine and ninety years, they are showing increased confusion and dementia.

Last week we assisted them in selling their car and making plans for alternative transportation because my father-in-law was unable to renew his driver's license. We also set up a system of someone else taking responsibility for administering necessary medicines to my mother-in-

law. Neither she, her husband of sixty-four years, or both of them together can now manage the right number of the right pills at the right time.

These losses of independence and control may seem inevitable, but they still cause grief, both to them and their extended family.

And our dog, Mimi, a black Labrador nearly fifteen years old, was diagnosed less than three weeks ago with cancer. It grew unbelievably quickly and she died yesterday.

At the same time, we have more routine changes, losses, and grief going on. Our children and several other young adults come and go with frequent changes between our home, universities, jobs, apartments, relationships, goals, and interests. One of my brothers-in-law retired a few months ago and a sister-in-law is learning to cope with a newly diagnosed chronic illness.

This is life—the only constant is change.

And like everyone else, we have to adjust to change.

In various settings over many years I have worked with grief—my own and that of others. For nearly twenty years I have worked in hospice care as a nurse and educator; and before that I held a variety of nursing and nursing education positions in England, Tanzania, the United States, Lesotho, and Sierra Leone. More recently I have addressed issues related to death and grief in short-term consulting work in the United States and several other countries. I assisted with the development of a hospice program in Jordan, gave workshops for hospice and other health care professionals in Japan, and facilitated training programs and retreats for AIDS counselors in Uganda.

Often I am asked, "Do people in the USA, or the UK, or Uganda, or Jordan, or Japan, or Croatia, experience grief the same way?" The question cannot be answered definitely, as many variables can affect how any individual grieves. *However, my experiences lead me to think we all have much in common. Familiarity with death, role models, cultural traditions, religious beliefs, and the expression of grief may vary, but the pain we feel when someone we love dies is probably very similar no matter who we are or where we are from. We are all human and we all grieve.*

Time and again, when caring for those who are dying or grieving, or when teaching others to do this kind of care, I have been reminded—by people's reactions and comments—of the importance of knowing about the process of grieving and healing. In some ways people find the topic of grief familiar, because everyone has some experience with loss. In other ways, grief is strange and difficult, because most people have little knowledge of the process we need to go through to find peace. This knowledge does not take away the pain of loss, but it can help us understand what is happening, and that in itself helps. The knowledge may then lead us to develop skills to help ourselves and others as we work though our grief.

My husband's response to his diagnosis was to develop a plan of action. He gathered incredible amounts of information from organizations, the Internet, medical journals, newspaper articles, books, friends, colleagues, and medical experts, and determined the advantages and disadvantages of different treatment options. His active search for relevant knowledge led to his informed decision to reject the most commonly recommended treatment in favor of one that seems best for him. Gathering information also meant a chance to discuss what was happening, which has helped "normalize" his experience. And, he has received support from family, friends, and colleagues. Some of these people he expected to be supportive, others have been heartwarming surprises.

Solutions to his parents' changing needs were not difficult to identify or to establish. What took time and energy and love was being patient and gentle as they worked through the grief of their losses. Then they could consider various options and adjust to the changes.

The death of the dog seems trivial compared with the death of a person, but she was a part of our family, and so was her illness and death. We relearned the importance of open discussion of serious illness, the value of family communication, the comfort found in reminiscing, and the satisfaction of rituals to help mark the transition. Our burial ceremony may not impress anyone else, but it certainly helped us.

•

Perhaps the most valuable lesson about loss and grief is one that I have been fortunate enough to learn from experience, that I teach often, and that I relearn whenever I grieve: When we are grieving there is immeasurable value in the gift of presence—someone who will keep us company in our grief.

•

Those who offer their loving, quiet presence can be a welcome support when we grieve, and being able to offer that presence ourselves can be a important goal for us all to strive for.

I hope you receive the gift of presence for yourself from others when you are grieving, and find it in yourself to give to others who grieve. In that presence we can find comfort and, eventually, some healing of our grief.

172

Index

INDEX

death:
  accepting reality of, 38, 47–56,
    59
  from AIDS, *see* HIV/AIDS
  being present at time of, 50–51
  of employee, 137–39
  "forgetting," 31, 38, 52–53
  guilt about, 24, 30, 103
  parents' difficulty in talking
    about, 96–98
  relief at, 29–30, 40
  and returning to work, 130–33
  shielding children from, 96–97
  sudden vs. expected, 48–49, 89,
    138, 162
  teaching children about, 102,
    107–8
  telling story of, 51–52, 55, 64,
    112, 115
  violent, 24, 89, 115, 162; *see
    also* murder; suicide
depression, chronic, 115
disbelief, as stage of grief, 37–38,
  80, 113
drug use, 62, 86, 151, 153

eating, 30, 53, 112, 114, 126, 155
Employee Assistance Program
  (EAP), 59–61, 133, 135, 138,
  140, 161
exhaustion, 25, 30, 46, 79

Golden, Tom, 164
grief, grieving:
  age and, 90, 98–101, 150
  anticipatory, 49, 59, 139
  common reactions and feelings
    of, 24, 29–31, 53, 112–13,
    161, 171
  of coworkers, 136–38
  coworkers' reactions to, 130–33,
    136–37, 138
  difficult times in, 39–42

disproportionate reactions in, 71,
  74, 119
duration of, 35–44, 59, 85
and ethnic or cultural traditions,
  92–93
expectations about, 93, 119, 122
expected, 159–61
experience of, 27–33, 119
experiencing pain of, 57–65
as familiar and strange, 32–33,
  159, 171
first task of, 47–56, 58–59, 113
gender and, 90–91, 120
guilt and, 24, 30, 103
helpful response to, 64–65
helping colleague with, 133–35
helping employee with, 135–37
helping someone with, 117–27
helping yourself with, 111–16
immediate reactions of, 23–25
as individual response, 33, 39,
  51, 83–94, 112, 126
as journey, 32–33, 43
letting others help with, 114–15
listening to, 123
and maintaining health, 53–55,
  114, 126, 155
misguided attempts to help with,
  55, 62, 63–64, 78, 120–22,
  125
mixed emotions of, 29, 31, 79,
  85, 113
mood shifts in, 29, 31
others' responses to, 62, 93
and personal circumstances,
  90–93
previous experience of, 87–89
process of, 32, 39, 42–43, 45–56,
  80, 171
progress in, 42–43, 115, 126
recognizing feelings of, 112
second task of, 47, 58–65, 113
and sexual needs, 112

174